GIFTED EDUCATION

Identification and Provision

DAVID GEORGE

David Fulton Publishers

London

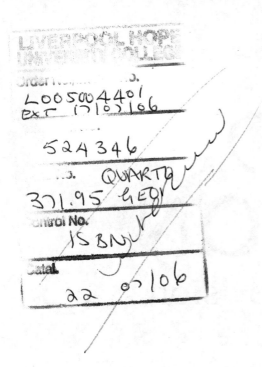
David Fulton Publishers Ltd
Ormond House, 26–27 Boswell Street, London WC1N 3JD
Web site: http://www.fultonbooks.co.uk

First published in Great Britain by
David Fulton Publishers 1995
Reprinted 1997, 1999, 2000

Note: The right of David George to be identified as the author of this work has been asserted by him in accordance with the Copyright, Designs and Patents Act 1988.

Copyright © David George

British Library Cataloguing in Publication Data

A catalogue record for this book is available from the British Library

ISBN 1-85346-347-7

Typeset by FSH, London
Printed in Great Britain by Bell & Bain Ltd., Glasgow

Contents

Dedication

This book is dedicated to our children who are tomorrow's world

Preface

This book is aimed at teachers and other professionals as well as parents concerned about the education of more able children, also known as gifted and talented children. It aims to assist the busy classroom teacher in becoming a more patient and observing teacher; giving them a knowledge base on which to work in defining their objectives in providing for these children; and to raise the awareness of teachers and parents that some of these children are under-achieving in our schools and therefore not reaching their considerable potential. The author maintains that many of these children have special needs and special problems. They also have special, sometimes immense, talent to give to society. We owe it to them to help cultivate their abilities, not only for their own sake but also for the good of society at large. Children are the most precious natural resource in the world and one that cannot be allowed to be squandered. Indeed the survival and achievements of the human species owe much to one characteristic – a capacity for creative problem solving, which many of these children possess.

There has been a growing interest in these children in recent years and, thanks to the Department for Education, together with NACE and NAGC, this movement is gaining momentum. There is also the challenge raised by OFSTED inspections: every report the author has seen mentions underachieving able children and the lack of differentiated lessons.

As we move towards the next century the mission of all teachers and parents should be to continue the search for powerful ways to provide appropriate education for the unique needs and abilities of gifted learners, and to bring the results of that search into general education to enable all children to reach their highest potential. This does not mean that all children should have the same educational experience, but there would be considerable spin-off from good practice, for all children in our schools.

This book discusses the problems of definitions, advocates a multi-dimensional approach to identification and, more importantly, how busy teachers can enrich, extend and differentiate the curriculum for these children. There is some discussion about the brain, teaching and learning as well as the most essential ingredient, which I call 'the affective curriculum'.

The author would like to express his warmest thanks to numerous colleagues who supported the writing of this book, several of whom have given permission to quote from their work, including those from schools where the author has worked. One of the great joys of giving many courses in schools is meeting devoted colleagues and children from whom I have learnt so much. These teachers, as well as members of NACE and NACG, have contributed in many ways through discussions and anecdotes about these children and their invaluable experiences with them. My sincere apologies to those who I may have inadvertently left out or not acknowledged in the text; this is inevitable when teachers are so keen and generous in giving me information. It is my hope in this book that all of you who care about gifted individuals will find much that will aid you to discover the excitement, challenge and pleasure of being with these special children as we share with them the process of growing up.

David George
Northampton
April 1995

CHAPTER 1

Definition

They are able because they think they are able. (Virgil)

One of the great challenges we face as teachers is the need to meet the individual intellectual, social and emotional needs of the children we teach. While the 1981 Education Act has provided a legal requirement for local education authorities to meet the needs of the least able, who are defined as those who are emotionally, behaviourally or intellectually of a lower level of attainment than their peers, it is equally the inalienable right of the more able to have their needs met by the provision of quality education. Thanks to the Department for Education's two conferences in the autumn of 1993, and the DFE circulars 4/93 and 5/93 for primary and secondary schools respectively, there is now some action to support work with our more able children. We would all agree that every child has the right to go as far and as fast along every dimension of the school curriculum as is necessary to reach their considerable potential, and this should be one of the major aims of education.

Why should we address this issue? There are a number of reasons why we need to give careful thought to the needs of the more able child:

● I suggest that all pupils possess the right to have their needs met by the teaching they receive. However, there is plenty of evidence from HMI and OFSTED reports of numbers of children underachieving. The increased frequency of school inspection and greater emphasis placed on accountability mean that we must have a policy in place which reflects the strategies we are adopting to meet individual needs. By implementing such strategies we should develop a range of teaching and learning styles which will meet the needs of all abilities and, in so doing, improve the quality of our provision.

● Any able children, if not extended and enriched by the education they are receiving, frequently resort to anti-social behaviour. Meeting the needs of these children will help to improve behaviour both in school and in society at large.

● By failing to extend more able children and help them reach their true potential, we are contributing to an enormous waste of talent for the community and the economy as a whole. All talent should be used for the benefit of the person and of society.

Information related to these individuals who possess superior characteristics in one or more areas should be included in any discussion of exceptional children. These children are referred to as gifted and talented, and require special education that provides them with an opportunity to develop those superior skills.

Until this century, individuals were identified as gifted only after they had made significant contributions to society. Sir Frances Galton, Albert Einstein and Thomas Edison are a few examples of gifted individuals identified in this way. There are limitations, however, in the identification of individuals as gifted by using this method. For example, it eliminates most children from consideration because few will make significant contributions to society early in life, and it assumes that giftedness will emerge over time. More recently, definitions have focused on identifying children who have the *potential* to excel as well as those who have already demonstrated excellence in some area.

Historically we can go back further and trace our interest in the gifted to philosophers such as Socrates and Plato, who viewed giftedness as passing through stages of knowledge more quickly and achieving higher levels of understanding. The concept of gifted moved from the philosophical and rationalistic to a fixed intelligence concept. Galton (1869) was one of the first to try and construct an intelligence test. His efforts were mirrored by Binet who was commissioned to develop a test to isolate and identify slow school children. These two, along with Terman (1947), moved the concept of giftedness from one of philosophical and rational enquiry into a scientific enquiry into the differences of intellect.

Defining giftedness has progressed from a one-test and one-fixed-construct approach centering on intellectual giftedness to the concept of multiple talents or intelligences. This idea is reflected in the American definition, given below, which is used by many other countries around the world.

Neuroscience and cognitive psychology provide us with new insights into what it means for children and youth to be outstanding talents, and require us to develop a new definition of this population. The term 'gifted' connotes a mature power rather than a developing ability and, therefore, is antithetic to recent research findings about children. The following definition, based on that used in the US federal Javits Gifted and Talented Education Act (1993), reflects today's knowledge and thinking:

> Children and youth with outstanding talent perform or show the potential for performing at remarkably high levels of accomplishment when compared with others of their age, experience or environment.
>
> These children and youth exhibit high performance capability in intellectual, creative, and/or artistic areas; possess an unusual leadership capacity, or excel in specific academic fields. They require services or activities not ordinarily provided by the schools.
>
> Outstanding talents are present in children and youth from all cultural groups, across all economic strata, and in all areas of human endeavour.

To put this definition into practice, schools must develop a system to identify gifted and talented students.

Another popular definition offered by Renzulli (1977) consists of above average intelligence, task amendment, and creativity. However, this definition has narrow applicability to high-achieving students who, for example, demonstrate creativity only.

The particular definition adopted by an individual school in its policy for gifted and intelligent children is especially important because it will determine the children who will be involved in a special programme the school decides to implement. Terms often used in this country are able, more able, exceptional, talented, superior, gifted, higher educational potential, more receptive learners, more capable learners, high academic potential. In Britain we tend to have adopted the term 'more able', whatever that means, although at the conferences mentioned above, there were an enormous range of titles given to these children, some of which are used interchangeably. Identifying what is a more able child is no easy matter, as such children do not form a homogeneous group whose talents can be easily generalized. One of the earlier and foremost researchers in this county, Eric Ogilvie (1972), stated that to be gifted is to be outstanding in general or specific abilities in a relatively broad or narrow field of endeavour. He suggests that six areas could be considered:

physical talent
mechanical ingenuity
visual and performing abilities
outstanding leadership and social awareness
creativity
high intelligence.

In his research in England, Ogilvie identified 3 per cent of children as being broadly gifted across the whole curriculum, but 36 per cent as having individual or specific talents. These percentages are almost identical to that of the US Office of Education (Marland, 1971).

Each definition has its own individual appeal. The Cheshire Education Authority's definition, taking into account the National Curriculum, is as follows:

Gifted and talented children are those who are functioning at the end of that particular key stage or one key stage ahead, and whose abilities are so well developed and so far advanced of their peer group that a school has to provide additional learning experiences which develop, enhance and extend the identified abilities.

The theory of multiple talents or intelligences, to which Howard Gardner (1983) refers, means that there is no single identikit for use in identification. Therefore we should consider any child as more able who in any aspect of human potential or achievement is far more advanced beyond what we as professional teachers would expect of a child of that chronological age. For the purpose of this workbook, the following definition is adopted and is to be recommended:

Gifted students are those with a potential to exhibit superior performance across a range of areas of endeavour. Talented students are those with a potential to exhibit superior performance in one area of endeavour.

This definition is generally accepted throughout the world, although in Britain we still prefer 'more able'.

You may now pause to consider what one might mean by 'potential', and how that is determined; what 'superior' means; and why 'giftedness' cannot be ascribed to a single ability.

From this brief introduction it is obvious that definitions abound and create much confusion. Anyone who takes the trouble to delve into the mass of published material on this subject is likely to be startled, if not confused, by the variety of terms used to describe very able children and the various criteria used to define them. It is suggested that the terms used above for gifted and talented are probably the best available to our schools.

It is important to realize that gifted and talented students are not a homogeneous group. They do not all exhibit the same traits or characteristics, but rather a wide range of individual differences. No single trait itself constitutes giftedness. These children often exhibit superior abilities and task commitment, not necessarily in pro-social ways or within the school curriculum. Remember that children are only in schools for 17 per cent of their waking life, and teachers need to be cognisant of what goes on within the hidden curricula after school. Education does not stop at the school gates!

Children's gifts and talents may become apparent at different stages of their lives. A child may exhibit talents in one area, e.g. art or music, or in a combination of areas. These children are present in all groups in society, including those requiring remediation in certain subject areas. The debate continues and the jury is still out!

Before we conclude this opening section we need to consider a third category, and that is the child who is underachieving.

Underachievement

Underachievement is a discrepancy between a child's school performance and some index of his or her actual ability, or the performance in scholastic attainment which is substantially below predicted levels. Gifted children are at a high risk, both emotionally and psychologically, in that their unique intellectual and creative abilities make them vulnerable at home and school to pressures which may initiate underachievement. HMI reports frequently give evidence from school surveys of many children underachieving and not reaching their true potential (see, for example, DES, 1992).

The earlier definitions have frequently been based on test results which can be problematic when related to underachievement. As teachers, we can employ a range of alternative methods of identification which will provide information from various sources. Understanding the behaviour and recognizing the characteristics of underachievers are essential if we are then to provide a remedy.

Studies of gifted underachievers have identified characteristics that are typical of such children; they fall into three levels:

● low self–esteem

● academic avoidance behaviour

● poor study skills, poor peer acceptance and lack of concentration.

A profile of an underachiever would include the following:

- poor test performance
- orally knowledgeable but poor in written work
- superior comprehension and retention of concepts when interested
- apparently bored
- achieving below expectations in basic subjects
- restless or inattentive
- daily work often incomplete or poorly done
- dislikes practice work
- absorbed in a private world
- tactless and impatient of slower minds
- prefers friendship with older pupils or adults
- excessively self-critical
- unable to make good relationships with peer group and teachers
- emotionally unstable – low self-esteem, withdrawn and sometimes aggressive
- has wide range of interests and possibly an area of real expertise.

Finding a cure

The cure for underachievement lies in careful assessment, possibly by an educational psychologist; communication between pupil, teacher and parents; higher expectations; role model identification; correction of deficiencies; reinforcement and above all patience, dedication, and warm and encouraging support from both parents and teachers.

Butler-Por (1987) concludes that we should adopt a multi-dimensional approach to the problems of underachieving children, providing an appropriate educational environment in the classroom and utilizing teaching methods capable of answering children's needs, which can contribute towards reversing underachievement in young children of all ability levels. Since teachers often encounter difficulties in recognizing both the diversity of potential and the specific needs of underachievers in their classes, we should encourage both them and the parents of the children in their charge to understand better the capabilities, needs and behaviour of children, so that they can initiate the appropriate intervention and plan the kind of educational environment and learning experiences capable of breaking the cycle of failure in some children.

As we learn more about the characteristics of gifted and talented children, we find that many of them have been overlooked, for example, handicapped students, students from minority backgrounds and even some girls. Harvey and Steeley (1984) administered a battery of tests at a correctional centre and found 18 per cent were gifted. They also noted that the pattern of abilities was not consistent with classroom-related tasks. Clearly the need to identify special groups of giftedness in students is one of the greatest challenges facing those of us interested in this field.

Culturally different children are also difficult to identify. Coleman (1985) noted that the number of gifted students from non-white, non-middle class, non-urban backgrounds is disproportionately low. Identification amongst these types of students is difficult, because they typically score lower than average on traditional tests of intelligence and achievement. It is hard to find research to indicate why this is so. Some say that the tests themselves are biased, whereas others support the idea that these children score low because of the lack of opportunity to develop and grow intellectually. Here is a challenge for further research, but it is apparent that these students from minority groups or impoverished backgrounds have the potential if given the opportunity to achieve highly.

Gifted girls

The education of gifted girls has historically been largely ignored. In the workforce, women continue to be under-represented in the most traditional male professions, and salaries are comparatively poor. No country can afford to lose around 50 per cent of its national potential. Although in many countries gifts and talents of girls are being recognized, there is still a long way to go. Historically the main problem is the home/career conflict, and although there is no easy solution, some women decide in advance to compromise their career to fit husband and family needs.

Peer and social attitudes and expectations often depress female achievement, and school expectations reward male independence, confidence and aggressiveness, but reward female conformity. There is some evidence to suggest that some all-girl classes and schools may help some girls take leadership positions, as well as courses they might otherwise avoid such as mathematics and science. This special problem that characterizes the wide-reaching cultural underachievement of women requires that all persons be enlisted in the tasks of changing the culture in order to support the development of women. The rewards to individual girls and to our society as a whole will make the effort most worthwhile.

CHAPTER 2

Identification

The definition of gifted and talented students we have adopted indicates that they can possess superior capabilities in a number of areas including intellectual, academic, creative, social or leadership, and psychomotor. Indeed, the specific characteristics that compose the heterogeneous group known as gifted and talented are numerous, and individual students might display any combination of them.

Identification Procedure

Initial concern from parents teacher or pupil that a pupil may be exceptionally able or talented and that their curriculum needs may not be being fully met.

Question	Action	Purpose
What information do we have to make us believe this child has exceptional ability or talent?	Summarise all available information –educational history –parental –medical analyse reason for concern –peer/teacher view	To identify past observations or advantages to learning. To identify patterns of performance To clarify intuitive responses
Is our intuition borne out in performance?	Objective teacher observation based on an agreed structured framework	To provide a systematic record of current behaviour interests and aptitudes. Is performance affected by different situations?
What do our observations indicate? How should we proceed?	compare with a checklist of behavioural criteria (gifted and underachieving)	–to devise an individual profile –to identify possible under achievement
Have we enough information? (What else do we need to know and why? – see criteria for using test)	Select a standardised test – using criteria	To supplement the existing information and inform the planned action and curriculum provision
What do we do with this information?	Systematically and succinctly record the information	–for future reference –so there is a reference for future action planning –to give a rationale for future action planning
How do we meet the needs of this pupil?	–inform all involved (teachers/parents/pupils) –agree criteria for future performance –plan future action –agree a time to review	Common awareness. To provide curriculum planning

Request outside help at any point in this process but such requests should outline at what point on the continuum help is requested and why?

Figure 2.1 *Printed with permission from Cheshire LEA, after an Inset course*

Because of the various areas in which a student can be identified as either broadly gifted or more narrowly talented, it is not surprising that many sources of information are typically used to identify this population of children. Essentially, these can be categorized into three major areas: use of rating scales and checklists; the administration of different types of standardized test; and teacher appraisal.

The following are suggestions for the busy teacher to use in the classroom for identifying these children. You may like to consider the Cheshire Local Education Authority identification procedure chart shown in Figure 2.1, which will give you an overview of the issue.

Historically, the identification process for these children has been stimulated by a desire to gain more information about them in order to give them an appropriate educational programme; up to recently in the United Kingdom this has meant providing additional enrichment materials. First, however, as a school there is a need for teachers and administrators to agree on the type of giftedness being identified, and the measures used to screen and identify should be compatible with the student population and the programme you have in mind to provide.

Checklists and rating scales

We need to start early, and cooperation with the parents of the children is essential. Many schools now send a booklet, for example, entitled 'All About Me' to the parents to complete before the child comes to school. Some schools go further and visit the homes of children prior to coming to school, to get to know the children in advance. It has been estimated that 90 per cent of the brain cells by weight are laid down by the time the child is five; indeed, the Jesuits always seem to have known this and say 'Give me a child until he is seven and when he is old he will not depart therefrom'. Because of this knowledge about the brain, we now recognize that parents are the most important teachers a child ever has, so much has been done before the child enters school. Therefore, it is crucial that schools should know the baseline of these children as they enter the school, and give them programmes to fit accordingly.

Education in these early crucial years is not a watered down or simplified version of the curriculum of older children. A 4-year-old child is not an immature 5-year-old, but is an individual with particular needs and characteristics. A school's work is based on valuing and extending the experiences that children bring to a school. As these experiences are individual and different, each child is seen as unique and treated accordingly.

It is not always immediately obvious what children are achieving in the early years of school. The early years staff work with children on their own and in groups. Cooperation, collaboration, listening skills, independence, self-discipline and a love of learning are some of the skills and attitudes that are taught and encouraged, and parents need to understand this.

The early years staff observe individual children closely, record their development, and plan for their progress. They aim to help children to develop socially, emotionally, intellectually, physically, morally and creatively. They then try to match activities, experiences and interaction to each child, thereby meeting the special needs of all children. This is why a booklet or checklist for

INFANT CHECKLIST

This needs to be discussed with the parents of the child.

Did your child learn to talk and walk early?

Does your child appear to be unusually attentive and able to concentrate?

Does your child show advanced motor skills and is your child good at physical activities?

Is your child curious about the world, and keen on exploring and discovering its meaning?

Is your child really well above the age level in ability and even self-taught?

Is your child interested in the whys and the wheres as well as the hows?

Does your child have a good vocabulary?

Does your child show special abilities in such areas as problem solving, art, music or mathematics?

Is your child intense and preoccupied with issues and questions that other children ignore?

Does your child delight in the unexpected?

These are indicators, not labels, and are clearly not an exhaustive list. All children need support from both parents and teachers. A discussion with a child's teacher will help discover your child's level of ability and therefore provision of education.

parents to complete is so important in getting to know the child early; it enables teachers to start from and build on what has already been achieved. It also means that early signs of giftedness can be spotted; these can include the following:

● language proficiency, using phrases and entire sentences at a very early age

● the early use of large vocabulary, accurately employed; early development of reading

● keen observation and retention of information about things observed; ability to attend or concentrate for a longer period than is typical of most children

● demonstration of proficiency or early interest in drawing, music and other art forms

● interest in or liking for books and, later, dictionaries, encyclopaedias and atlases

● early discovery of cause and effect relationships

● keen sense of curiosity, fun and humour.

This list of characteristics can be grouped in terms of psychological concepts, but it should be kept in mind that the variables interact and that the samples are not representative of a full socio-economic range.

Checklists have been widely advocated to improve the efficiency of teacher judgement. They can be rather subjective with no indication of how well a child must score to be considered gifted. However, a checklist can prove helpful in alerting parents and teachers to the possibility that they may be misjudging some of their children, and it would encourage them to look for signs or talents which they may have failed to acknowledge. They can also influence strategies and open up a dialogue with children and parents. Many different checklists have been put forward, some fairly short and concise, others of great length and all-embracing detail. Below is a general checklist used by many schools in this country now; it can serve as a guide. None of the behaviours in the checklist should be taken as proof of high ability, but they can alert teachers and parents to the need to question the reasons for their occurrence. If a child measures up to quite a number of those listed – and the child in the completed checklist below certainly does – then you should enquire further into a child's abilities.

Child's Name: Mary Jones	Sex: F		Age: 9y 3m Date of Birth: 3.4.71		
Characteristic	**Poor**	**Weak**	**Average**	**Good**	**Exceptional**
Use of language					X
Reasoning ability					X
Speed of thought					X
Imagination				X	
Memory					X
Observation				X	
Concentration			X		
Whether questioning					X
Makes original suggestions				X	
Problem solving					X
Extent of reading					X
Routine work	X				

Subject checklists

It can be easy to identify able children: many able children cope well with normal classwork and stand out when given something different to do. Conversely though, ability is not always obvious, particularly in children who do not push themselves forward or who do not always have the opportunity to demonstrate their talents.

The majority of checklists derive from research into intelligence and creativity, but they have rarely been tested in the classroom for their validity. They may be comforting to some teachers, because they tend to confirm teachers' own estimations of their pupils' abilities and therefore are unlikely to yield the results for which they were originally designed.

There are now available subject-specific checklists, some examples are given below. Readers are referred to Denton and Postlethwaite's (1985) research in Oxfordshire where they used checklists to identify children in ten comprehensive schools in four subject areas.

The following list of characteristics is adapted from *Mathematics for Gifted Pupils* by Anita Straker (1983). The mathematically able:

- are better able to grasp the essence of a problem at once, or relate one problem to another quite different one
- can generalize mathematical material rapidly and easily
- tend to skip over intermediate steps in a logical argument
- strive for an elegant solution where possible
- reverse their train of thought if necessary
- tend to remember the relationships in a problem and the principles of a solution, whereas less capable pupils tend to remember only specific details, if anything, about a problem.

Some other behavioural characteristics noted by teachers which mathematically able pupils may display have been included in the following checklist, which also has questions related to other subjects. (Other examples of checklists can be found in George, 1992.)

We have a lot of bright children in our schools but not many who are gifted learners. The chart on page 13 may help you identify and distinguish these two categories and give you a better understanding of gifted children. Of course, if we give children the opportunity to contribute to their learning by flexible programming and the provision of a creative learning environment, who knows how many more would come into the gifted learner category?

MATHEMATICAL ABILITY CHECKLIST

Does the child display the following characteristics:

Persistence in a search for the best and simplest solution to a problem? Children who have a gift for mathematics do not easily tire when they are occupied with it. Eleven- or 12-year-old pupils, for example, can work continuously for up to three hours before showing any deterioration in their performance.

Self-confidence in a new mathematical situation, where they are prepared to use initiative in tackling something different? They make statements like, 'I know, I'll try so and so' or, 'No, that can't be right because...' or, 'Look, I'll show you'.

Open-mindedness? Mathematically capable children will weigh evidence and be prepared to change a point of view according to the evidence.

Perpetual posing of problems to themselves, during lessons and at home? For instance: 'How many people could stand on the Wembley Football pitch?', 'How many seconds does a person live in a lifetime?', 'What area can you see from the top of the Post Office Tower?', 'How fast is that aeroplane going?', etc.

Terse, even laconic expressions of thought? This may show itself in mathematics where there may be a dislike, in the early stages, of writing out solutions to problems which can be solved mentally; it can also manifest itself in written work in English.

Have a general interest in numbers (e.g., car numbers having special properties, 219 being divisible by 3, etc.)?

Have a general interest in patterns in shape?

Is often able to find shortcut solutions to problems, wanting to avoid standard methods?

SCIENTIFIC ABILITY CHECKLIST

Does the child think quickly and accurately?

Does he/she display curiosity and have wide interests, observe closely?

Does he/she, with minimum or no direction, pursue particular interests well beyond what is normally required?

Can he/she work happily on (a) an individual basis, (b) a small group basis?

In new situations is he/she able to use what he/she has learned within and outside the school?

Does the child display creativity or originality in any form of problem solving?

Does he/she, when stimulated, consider alternative ways of thinking about a problem (i.e., offer alternative hypotheses and different ways of arriving at a solution)?

Is he/she able to communicate his/her ideas?

CREATIVE WORKING CHECKLIST

Is the child particularly fluent in the use of written language generally?

Does the child show a genuine enthusiasm for writing stories, poems and/or dramatic dialogue? Does he/she produce surprising and unusual work from class projects, and continue to write in his/her own time?

Does he/she show an interest in language and literature and the kinds of playful experimentation that can be done with rhythm, metaphor, narrative, dialogue and the sounds of words?

Does he/she usually have something distinctive and personal to say about his or her own experience – something which shows that he/she uses writing to reflect on and explore experiences beyond the extent normally pursued by peers?

Would the child welcome the chance to work with others on writing, revising and performing? Do you feel that he or she would benefit from a brief change of setting, an extra stimulus and sustained work on writing over a three-day period?

ART ABILITY CHECKLIST

Does the child display the following characteristics:

A high level of curiosity about objects, ideas, situations and events?

An ability to fantasize?

A sensitivity to beauty?

A willingness to work for extended periods on a single theme?

A previously demonstrated tendency to express ideas through drawings or models?

Bright child	Gifted child
Is interested	Is highly curious
Answers the questions	Discusses in detail
Knows the answers	Asks the questions
Top set	Beyond the group
Grasps the meaning	Draws inferences
Is alert	Is keenly observant
Completes the work	Initiates projects
Has good ideas	Has unusual and silly ideas!
Enjoys school	Enjoys learning
Good memory	Good guesser
Is pleased with learning	Is highly critical
Is receptive	Is intense
Learns easily	Already knows
Enjoys straightforward sequential presentation	Thrives on complexity
Enjoys peers	Prefers adults or older pupils
Absorbs information	Manipulates information

Bright children are often the 'teacher pleasers', and certainly easier and a pleasure to teach. Gifted children can be extremely difficult because they do not fit the norm.

Rating scales

These are more soundly constructed than the more subjective general checklists, and contain sub-scales such as creativity, leadership, motivational and learning characteristics, which can be highly correlated with one another and with other objective measures of the characteristics of gifted children. Readers are referred to the gifted behaviour index written by Dr Judy Eby and published by DOK New York, which includes rating scales for maths, science and problem solving, musical ability, visual and spatial ability, social and leadership ability, and mechanical, technical and inventiveness ability. Another well-known rating scale is that produced by Renzulli and Hartmann (1971); a sample is printed below. This instrument is designed for teacher use without further training, and includes 37 items. The authors reviewed the literature on the traits of gifted and talented students before deciding on the items to be included in the rating scale. Teachers are required to rate a student on each of the 37 items, using the following guidelines and scores:

1 – If you have seldom or never observed this behaviour.

2 – If you observe this behaviour occasionally.

3 – If you observe this behaviour to a considerable degree.

4 – If you observe this behaviour almost all the time.

Unfortunately the authors do not really define the terms such as 'occasionally' and 'considerable degree', nor do they offer any cut-off points. A child who is being considered for an enrichment programme for example, whose eligibility criteria include a high IQ, would probably score high on the learning characteristic section as having quick mastery and recall of factual information. Nevertheless the rating scale is recommended and it certainly is more quantifiable than the normal checklist discussed earlier.

CREATIVITY CHARACTERISTICS *Score*

1. Generates a large number of ideas or solutions to problems and questions; often offers unusual way out, unique, clever responses.

2. Is uninhibited in expressions of opinion; is sometimes radical and spirited in disagreement; is tenacious; is a high risk taker; is adventurous and speculative.

3. Displays a keen sense of humour and sees humour in situations that may not appear to be humourous to others.

4. Is sensitive to beauty; attends to aesthetic characteristics of things.

LEARNING CHARACTERISTICS

1. Possesses a large storehouse of information about a variety of topics.

2. Has quick mastery and recall of factual information.

3. Tries to understand complicated material by separating it into its respective parts; reasons things out for himself (sic); sees logical and commonsense answers.

4. Is a keen and alert observer; has unusually advanced vocabulary which he uses in a meaningful way.

LEADERSHIP CHARACTERISTICS

1. Participates in most social activities connected with the school and can be counted on to be there if anyone is.

2. Carries responsibility well; can be counted on to do what he has promised and usually does it well.

3. Is self-confident with children his own age as well as adults; seems comfortable when asked to show his work to the class.

4. Seems to be well liked by his classmates.

5. Can express himself well; has good verbal facility and is usually well understood.

MOTIVATIONAL CHARACTERISTICS

1. Needs little external motivation to follow through in work that initially excites him.

2. Is usually bored with routine tasks.

3. Becomes absorbed and truly involved in certain topics or problems; is persistent in seeking task completion.

4. Is interested in many adult problems such as religion, politics, world problems – more than usual for age level.

Table 2.1   *Examples from Renzulli's rating scale (reprinted with permission)*

Testing

During the past few years the introduction of the National Curriculum and national assessment, together with local and devolved school management, have brought about increased accountability in our schools. Assessment is now in the forefront of both educational thinking and parental concern. It is hoped that, where teachers' professionalism is held in increasingly high esteem, then assessment is skilfully integrated into the learning process of all our children. Amongst the wide range of tools now available to teachers as they encourage and enable children to fulfil their potential, assessment will be seen as particularly useful and reliable, and therefore meriting serious consideration.

Like many other types of exceptional children, gifted and talented individuals are frequently identified through the use of standardized tests. These instruments measure skills that are directly related to the classification of a gifted student, and throughout the world the results from group intelligence and group achievement tests are still used together to identify correctly some 96 per cent of students who have been classified as gifted. This is not surprising, when one considers that entry into most programmes for gifted children is based on superior performance on an individual intelligence test, usually one that is verbally based. Non-verbal test such as the Ravens Progressive Matrices have also been shown to be helpful in identifying gifted students. Similarly, most gifted students also perform well on tests of academic achievement, since it is typically superior classroom performance that is a reason for their referral in the first place.

Broad-based assessment is necessary in order to gauge performance, potential and progress. As a teacher, your professional expertise, observation skills and instincts all enable you to assess informally a pupil's level of attainment, though teachers are not so good at this as one would have hoped. More formal assessments are nevertheless useful to you, as objective results gained from the appropriate test will either confirm your initial impressions or encourage you to modify them in the light of the new objective evidence. You will also be able to present the unbiased test results as evidence of high ability.

Assessments contribute to education at every level and in many different ways. From simple baseline assessments for infants, discussed earlier, to state examinations at 16, their purposes vary but most are complementary to teaching strategies.

The National Curriculum and the 5 to 14 test have dominated recent debates, and some teachers believe that as they have to use national tests known as Standard Assessment Tasks anyway, these should tell them all they need to know about their pupils, and any other tests are unnecessary. A common misconception is that the national tests are standardized norm-referenced tests; they are in fact criterion-referenced. Although they can provide you with valuable information at the end of each key stage, they cannot tell you how well individual children are performing in relation to the true average level for their age.

From the discussion so far, teachers will realize that a wider range of assessments is necessary for several different reasons, not least in order to identify the various talents that these children seem to have. Current thinking may be that the average level for a 7-year-old is level two; however, only a norm-referenced test can tell you the true average level. Results obtained from a norm-referenced test may be compared with the national samples on which the test had been standardized, to show how an individual pupil is performing against his or her peer group nationally. In the field of gifted education the case for using norm-referenced tests is particularly strong when baseline assessment is required, such as when children enter a new school. It has already been emphasized that 5-year-olds entering infant school, for example, will have covered little prescribed or statutory curriculum work, yet may already be reading. Only their potential and aptitude in particular areas can be tested, and norm-referenced tests will best fulfil this function. Used in conjunction with criterion-referenced tests, they can provide schools with baseline evidence about each child, helping teachers to identify children's needs and target their teaching accordingly. This is crucial, because it is well known that if a child is bored, not appreciated, and is underachieving for a while, then it is difficult to motivate them again. Increasingly, schools need this kind of information not only to provide evidence of their effectiveness, but more especially to plan teaching programmes. The OFSTED report, *Access and Achievement in Urban Education* (1993) reveals that teachers are sometimes unaware of the range of ability within their classes.

The use of norm-referenced and criterion-referenced baseline tests in conjunction with national tests allows you to demonstrate the value-added component that your school has delivered, making any national test results more meaningful. For example, criterion-referenced baseline assessment such as the early years Easy Screen published by NFER-Nelson and a norm-referenced test such as a Larr test of emergent literacy, could be used to assess children on entry to primary school.

Tests are not constructed with the intention of children being able to get every item correct, although many able children will. Depending on the difficulty level of a particular test, they may only be required to score 50 per cent to be performing at the established mean or average level for their age. You may also be pleasantly surprised to find that a pupil does better than you expected, and often gifted and talented children enjoy these tests. One of the major benefits of using a suitable test is that it can provide you with objective evidence. It is very easy for us to let our judgements be influenced by our own subjective feelings and past experiences: so often there appears to be an expectation gap between how teachers think their pupils will react to the test, and how pupils actually do perform. Indeed, another problem we have in education is low expectations from some parents of their children. Therefore it is very important when designing, trialling and standardizing tests to ensure that children feel comfortable with them and are sufficiently motivated to do their best.

As to the choice of test, this is a difficult one as there are so many available, but Table 2.2 gives a variety of well-tried tests which are all published by NFER-Nelson, and are recommended. It is good to keep in mind that a criterion-referenced test will tell you what an individual pupil knows and can do, whereas a norm-referenced test will tell you how individual pupils are performing in relation to their age-related peers. If put to proper use, both kinds of information can greatly benefit pupils by ensuring easier differentiation of work at suitable levels for the individual, and by providing a measure of the national average performance. As has been indicated earlier, we need a wide range of information about these children in order to build up a complete profile of the child and then give the correct provision. In the author's experience, the AH Series of tests are the most successful in identifying these children, and certainly the most widely used. For further reference, teachers are recommended to read *Educational Assessment – the Way Ahead* (1994).

Title	Type	Age Range
Cognitive Abilities Test (CAT)*	Verbal, non-verbal and quantitative reasoning	8 – 15
NFER-Nelson Verbal Reasoning Series	Verbal reasoning	8 – 13
NFER-Nelson Non-Verbal Reasoning Test Series	Non-verbal reasoning	5 – adult
AH Series*	Non-verbal, verbal, numerical, perceptual	5 – adult
Raven's Progressive Matrices and Vocabulary Scales	Verbal and non-verbal reasoning	5 – adult
NFER-Nelson Special Access Test Series	Verbal and non-verbal reasoning, English and maths	11 +
NFER-Nelson Item Bank	Verbal and non-verbal reasoning, English and maths	11 +
Richmond Test of Basic Skills (2nd Edn)	Vocabulary, language, study skills, maths	8 – 14
British Picture Vocabulary Scale (BPVS)	Vocabulary	$2\frac{1}{2}$ – adult
*Possibly the best for these children		

Table 2.2 *Tests suitable for the identification of able children (NFER-Nelson)*

In most countries, IQ is one of the major criteria used to determine giftedness. In general, the cut-off point used is an IQ that is at least two standard deviations above average. This would indicate that individuals scored higher than 98 per cent of the population. Since most intelligence tests have a standard deviation of 15, this means a person would have to have an IQ of 130 or better. However, in addition to this high numerical score several other intellectual characteristics have been associated with gifted and talented students, and these include advanced logical thinking such as the ability to question, and problem-solving behaviour, as well as early language development.

Academic ability is perhaps the major reason why gifted and talented students are initially identified, at least within the school setting, as such abilities quickly gain the attention of the classroom teacher. It is obvious from these results that a child can be identified as performing above the average in academic subjects, but many other characteristics have to do with a gifted student's approaches to a task, study skills and application of the course content – gifted is as gifted does. For example, Bloom (1982) in his large-scale study of the characteristics of gifted children found that many engaged in solitary academic activities for long periods of time, and as well as having the ability to ask many questions, could make use of the answers, learn through observation, and had the ability to learn independently. (See the infant checklist discussed earlier for other characteristics.) This does not mean, however, that all children who learn early are gifted. There is plenty of evidence for late developers, especially boys. Some children are referred to as gifted underachievers, as we discussed earlier, and require a multi-dimensional identification approach as well as education programmes based on their individual needs.

Creativity

An area in which gifted and talented students often excel is creativity. Unfortunately, creativity is an extremely difficult concept to define and subsequently to measure. Some of the more interesting work in the area of creativity has been conducted by Paul Torrence (1980), author of a test called the 'Torrence Test of Creative Thinking'. As a result of his work with creative individuals, he developed a checklist of characteristics which includes the ability to express feelings and emotions, enjoyment of and skills in group activities, problem solving, the use of humour, and originality and persistence in problem solving. In addition to intelligence and achievement, this is another area which comes under our broad definition which needs to be identified. However, there is not necessarily a correlation between intelligence and creativity. The Torrence Test of Creative Thinking has two forms: verbal and figural. The students are required to do such things as suggest improvements in toys, complete unfinished pictures, and name unusual uses for common objects such as a bucket, a brick, or a newspaper. Each aspect of this test is designed to measure four areas: fluency, flexibility, originality and elaboration.

By including children with this particular talent area, we have therefore had a broadening effect on attitudes towards the gifted, and it is partly responsible for the reduction of elitism of which we are often accused.

Urban and Jellen (1988) state that high creativity is seen as the ability to create a new, unusual and surprising product by perceiving, processing and utilizing a maximum of available information. Clarke (1988) has elaborated an integral model of creativity consisting of four major dimensions: thinking, which involves sensing and solving problems and the use of divergent thinking ability; feeling, which focuses on the emotional wellbeing and self-actualizing of children (by this means we can encourage a change of attitude of mind – if you think well of yourself you can meet your creative potential); third, the intuitive components employ imagery, fantasy and impulses; and fourth, the sensing attribute involves a high level of mental and physical development resulting in inventions and products in talent areas. However, three caveats to this should be noted here:

1. Not all creative thinkers exhibit all the traits mentioned.
2. It is characteristics of thinking and cognitive style that guarantee creativity.
3. Children may have different faces and forms for different age groups as well as different cultural and social backgrounds.

The author recommends the Urban and Jellen Test for Creative Thinking – Drawing Production (1995) which is now being used in many schools in Britain. In this test, in order to achieve a high degree of culture fairness, Urban and Jellen decided to avoid verbal clues by choosing a drawing task instead with certain figural stimuli. These fragments of the drawing were intentionally designed in an incomplete fashion with no or only vague conventional meanings in order to achieve a maximum of flexibility as an imperative for creativity. As readers can see from Figure 2.2, this test for creative thinking is a drawing production test; the following criteria are included:

different in design
geometric and non-geometric
round and straight
single items for expansion
broken and unbroken
within and outside a given frame

A famous artist was called away to the phone having just begun a new creation. He never returned to it. How would his finished work have looked? You have fifteen minutes to complete it and give it a title.

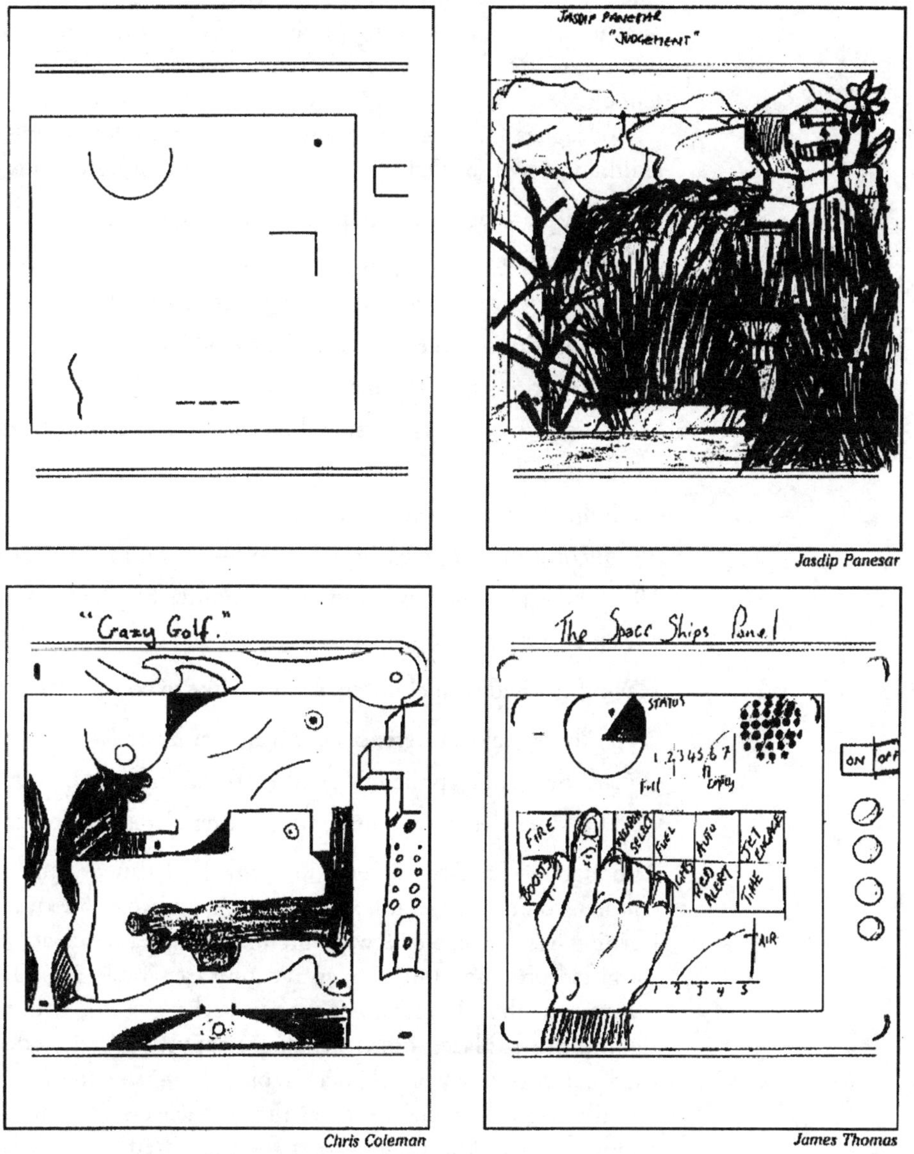
"Judgement"
Jasdip Panesar
"Crazy Golf."
Chris Coleman
The Space Ships Panel
STATUS
FIRE
ON
James Thomas

Figure 2.2 *Urban and Jellen test, 1995, Year 7 aged 11 years;* reproduced from *Test for Creative Thinking – Drawing Production.*

placed irregularly on the space provided

incomplete

Teachers simply say to the children that there was once a famous artist doing this drawing who was called away on urgent business and never went back to finish the drawing. You then ask the children to complete the drawing and give it an appropriate title. If children ask any questions these are not to be answered; you just ask them to do the two things. However, for your benefit you will note that there are five fragments inside the box and one outside to the right. One of the characteristics of gifted children is they take risks and break barriers; some children will move outside of the box and others will feel constricted by it.

The 11 evaluation criteria chosen for this test reflect an openness to experience and explore the six fragments in and outside the box. In order to avoid a culture bias, the researchers used only a drawing task with no verbal clues, and they state that high creativity can be seen as the ability to create a new, unusual and surprising product by perceiving, processing and utilizing all the fragments. The author has tested many children, and so have numerous schools.

Colleagues may like to try assessing the samples completed by 10-year-old children, shown in Figure 2.2. The 11 criteria to assess this test are:

1. continuations – extension of the six fragments

2. completions – additions to the extensions

3. new elements, new additions, figures or symbols

4. connections – lines between the elements

5. connections made to make a theme

6. boundary breaking outside the box, indicating risk taking

7. perspective

8. indications of a sense of humour

9. unconventional, e.g., turning the paper round – abstract

10. speed – allow a maximum of 15 minutes for the test

11. an appropriate title.

Having assessed your children, you may like to consider the following questions:

Are there major differences between genders?

Can the test be applied to children from different countries and cultures?

What does the test tell us about children's creative ability?

Although we in Britain tend to think that our system of education allows children to be creative, for example by the writing of essays, art work, discovery learning in science, etc., few programmes emphasize creativity as the focal point for gifted programming or identification (see Table 2.3). Too little emphasis is placed on the development of creativity in all children, and even less significance is placed on identifying creatively gifted students. It is important that not too heavy a reliance is placed on the more traditional means of identification discussed so far, as this will leave significant numbers of creative children out of the programmes for the gifted. The situation becomes even more critical when we consider the great strengths of disadvantaged and culturally different students, as they are often very creative and motivated. Nearly everyone recognizes or knows what creativity is generally, but there is less agreement on precise definitions and identification instruments (see Guilford's list, below). Observations of students engaged in problem-solving situations, and evaluations of students' work and performance are two means utilized to identify creatively gifted children; however, the above test is a recommended starting point. Challenges to creatively gifted children will be discussed later.

---

1. Listening to students
2. Flexibility in the curriculum
3. Encouraging thinking skills
4. Appreciating individuality and openness
5. Encouraging open discussion
6. Promoting active learning
7. The encouragement of frequent writing and especially reading of quality books
8. Accepting student ideas
9. Allowing time to think
10. Flexibility when children start school and move on from key stage to key stage, from school to university
11. Nurturing confidence
12. Giving helpful feedback – appreciating students' ideas
13. Encouraging students to join extramural activities such as Clubs, Societies and competitions
14. Bringing specialist mentors into school.

Table 2.3 *Aids to creativity*

Guilford (1959) states that creativity includes the following aptitudes along with being sensitive to problems and the ability to redefine and elaborate (I have added some examples to amplify his points):

Fluency – quantity; the ability to generate many solutions or alternatives. For example:
 Think of several possible ways to...
 Come up with ideas for...
 List as many ways to...

Flexibility – thinking in a variety of categories and taking several approaches. For example:
 Think of different kinds of reasons for...
 List as many different ways to...
 What are the different kinds of...

Originality – the ability to arrive at novel, unusual, non-conforming conclusions – uniqueness. For example:
 Think of unique and unusual ways to...
 Think of ideas no one else will think of...

Elaboration – the ability to add details and develop ideas. For example:
 Think of details to develop your ideas...
 Add supplementary ideas to make the basic idea clearer...

Figure 2.3 *A piece of music written by Philip, an autistic 10-year-old*

Musical ability in children

It is generally recognized that creativity tests or intelligence tests do not necessarily identify students who are talented in music. However, the Arnold Bentley Test for Music is recommended. It could be maintained that a certain degree of intelligence is required to understand and carry out the instructions of many tests, but in order to reduce to a minimum any such demand on intelligence, as distinct from the musical abilities we are seeking to measure, much care was taken over instructions for this test. Children and adults are tested in four areas: pitch discrimination, tonal memory, rhythmic memory and chord analysis. The author recently tested an autistic 10-year-old boy who scored the maximum marks on both tunes and rhythm, with 14 out of 20 for pitch and 19 out of 20 for chords. This child has a unique talent in music only, and is composing music comparable with the output of any A-level music student. His total score for the test was 53 out of 60 marks, which is certainly as good as the choral scholars and music graduates tested by Bentley. Figure 2.3 shows a piece of music written by Philip which is technically correct, written in a difficult key and time scale.

As a successful outcome of this test, the author found a mentor for Philip, a head of music department who was just about to retire, and who now has a half-day with Philip once a month to encourage him and teach him to improve his music. They have worked on a piece of music for a school orchestra, and are now working on music for the County Youth Orchestra. This child deserves to go to a special school for young musicians, but because of lack of parental support and finances, is unable to do so. Here is an example of the underprivileged in our society, and possibly one out of many who just do not have the opportunity to go as far as they possibly can. What a terrible waste of talent!

Teacher judgement and nomination

It is obvious that teachers play an important role in the identification of gifted and talented children. Teachers ought to know their children and their abilities; it is frequently the teacher that first notices some area in which a child is excelling. Many screening programmes for gifted children rely heavily on teacher referral. It is unfortunate, however, that most attempts to determine the efficiency of teacher judgement have produced somewhat negative results. In what has become a classic study, Pegnato and Birch (1959) reported that teachers are not good at identifying gifted students in their classrooms. Researchers had previously identified gifted students with IQs of 136 or above, then had applied several criteria including teacher judgement to identify the gifted students. To their surprise they found that teachers only referred 45 per cent of those identified by tests as gifted; only 31 per cent of those identified by the teachers had average IQs.

The author and others have shown that teacher judgement can be greatly improved by in-service training. In a recent survey (NAGC, 1995) of 130 schools where the author had undertaken in-service training on gifted and talented education, 78 per cent of the schools said, amongst other things, that they now had a positive identification policy and that far more teachers were now correctly identifying gifted and talented children. It is probable that the training helped to eliminate some of the ambiguity about the nature of giftedness, especially as the author stresses a multi-dimensional approach, looking at all talents and not just the academic.

In a surprising piece of research, Coleman (1985) reported that he found that teachers had more difficulty in identifying younger children than older secondary-age children. It was also noted that the more mixed the ethnic and racial composition of the class, the more difficult it was for teachers to identify giftedness. It seems reasonable to expect that primary school teachers in Britain would know their children particularly well, because most teachers teach the whole class for most of the time, whereas in the secondary school, where teachers specialize, they are likely to teach 300 different children in any one school week. In Britain, Denton and Postlethwaite (1985) undertook a thorough piece of research on identification in 11 Oxfordshire comprehensive schools, where they tried to identify the top 10 per cent in four specific subject areas, namely mathematics, physics, English and French. In English and mathematics there was a high level of agreement between teacher-based assessments of pupils with high ability in subject-specific, test-based measures, but the teachers missed some high-scoring pupils and included some low scorers, whereas in French and physics there was enough mismatch between the teacher and test-based assessments to show errors of judgement by teachers. Researchers used a variety of tests as well as subject-specific checklists and teacher nomination. Their study concludes:

- there are benefits in using other teachers as second observers in the classroom situation
- the importance of accurate subject-specific checklists should be passed on from year group to year group
- to develop strategies that provide challenging work to enable children to show their abilities rather than using tests
- use a variety of teaching styles and particularly give children opportunities to work together in small groups for free discussion
- children give off signals as to their ability, once they are given the opportunity to show that ability; that depends on the teaching style adopted by teachers. Children need to be given the opportunity to do work at their level and beyond that level, and thereby stop repetitive practice which leads to boredom.

Other considerations

Space does not allow for more detailed identification procedures for the other talent areas such as leadership or psychomotor skills, but readers are referred to George (1992) for more information.

Other considerations in order to build up a complete profile of the child are self nomination, parent nomination, and peer group nomination.

Above all, it is important to understand our children in all their attributes, especially with our broad definition of multiple talents in mind. It will not take many minutes for a teacher to complete a pupil pro forma such as the one shown in Figure 2.4, which helps to build up an holistic view of an individual child.

Pupil's name:	Age:	Form:
Item	**Characteristic and abilities**	

1. Academic performance
Strengths **and** weaknesses e.g. 'outstanding at mathematics'; 'can cope with logarithms in her year'; 'Grade VIII pianist at 11 years'; 'motor cooordination poor'; 'written and drawn work messy'; 'reading age three years above chronological age'; 'exceptional vocabulary for age'; 'much quicker than I am'

1.
2.
3.
4.
5.

2. Personal interests
Record all known hobbies and enthusiasms including comments on time spent on them and levels of knowledge gained, e.g. 'plays chess at local adults' club'; 'outstanding left half with boys' county team'; two evenings per week at St John's Ambulance, with advanced first aid certificate'; etc

1.
2.
3.
4.
5.

3. Extracurricular (school-based) activities
'Form captain'; 'junior eleven cricketer'; 'goalkeeper – hockey team'; 'school choir, drama group film club, ornithology club', 'rushes straight home after school each night'

1.
2.
3.
4.
5.

4. School relations and personality
'Recluse'; 'is bullied as being teacher's pet'; 'extrovert'; 'social star'; 'often organizes a group of classmates in the laboratory'; 'no one will sit with her'; 'friendly, relaxed pupil'; 'popular without being assertive'

1.
2.
3.
4.
5.

5. Physical description
'Healthy/unhealthy'; 'alert'; 'energetic'; nature of health problems, if any; 'neat, tidy'; 'physically advanced/retarded/normal for age'; level of coordination, etc.

1.
2.
3.
4.
5.

6. Home background
Parental occupations; socio-economic background; relations with parents, if known; other children in family and relations with them; information about child's behaviour at home, etc.

1.
2.
3.
4.
5.

Figure 2.4   *Pupil pro forma (adapted from Kerry, 1983)*

A pupil pro forma will help to build up a case study, which is another useful technique for identification of gifted and talented children. In working with a case study technique teachers must use the whole picture concept of giftedness, with as much data as possible collected in the child's file. An example would be the Record of Achievement now used in many secondary schools; this should include representative samples of a child's work, a summary of past educational experiences and achievements, anecdotal information, and methods of teaching used to meet the student's educational needs. (For more details of this technique please see Leyden, 1990, and George, 1992.)

A school adopts a referral form, such as the one shown in Figure 2.5, which is then given to the person in the school with responsibility for these children and with the authority to take appropriate action.

I wish to draw your attention to . . . .

in . . . . *(Class or Tutor Group)*

Please find attached the following:

1.   Checklist

2.   My written description of the child's classroom performance

3.   Letter from parent

4.   Test results

5.   Photocopied evidence from the child's written work

6.   Other

Signed. . . . .

Figure 2.5   *Referral form for gifted, talented or underachieving children*

Special groups of gifted children

The ineffectiveness and inefficiency of certain standardized tests in identifying culturally different children who are gifted or talented have been studied in the USA, but nothing has been done about these children, nor those from lower socio-economic classes in Britain. It is important that we concentrate on the subjective aspect of identification of the culturally different, many of whom have positive skills such as the following:

● high motivation in games, music and sport
● language rich in imagery
● ability in visual art
● high creativity in movement and dance, i.e. a fluency and originality.

The creativity tests mentioned earlier could be useful in identifying some of these aspects. Many of these children, it is suggested, need counselling (as do their parents) in order to build a comprehensive profile of a potentially gifted child, gathering information from parents, peers and teachers, as well as from the child concerned.

Once a child has been identified as being broadly gifted or having a particular talent, the dilemma then for the school is what is done to help that child reach their maximum potential. One suggestion is to use a referral form which all staff have in their possession. These should be completed and given to someone in the school who has the authority to take action in providing for the child identified.

Conclusion

From the foregoing it is obvious that every child is unique, and displays his or her giftedness in a unique way. For this reason it is difficult to define the concept or to define general characteristics according to which a child could be classified in a specific category of giftedness. It is obvious that a distinction must be made between specific and general giftedness, between intellectual and academic giftedness and talent, as well as between different kinds of giftedness like the gifted underachiever, the culturally different, and the disabled child. It is also recognized now that we must look at a wide talent pool. Renzulli's (1988) definition allows for a much larger group of pupils to be regarded as potentially gifted; if his three areas are in step and in focus, the person displays giftedness in performance. Certain people behave in this way at certain times and in certain situations. Certainly it is now recognized that giftedness is the potential for exceptional development of specific abilities as well as the demonstration of performance at the upper end of a talent continuum. This is not limited by age, gender, race, socio-economic status, or ethnicity.

Giftedness is undoubtedly a very vague and difficult concept to define for the different categories we have just discussed. It has a different meaning for different people in different countries. The author met children in Kenya who were superb ecologists. One boy knew by name each cow in a herd of 200, his memory and its application signifying an outstanding aptitude for the rural life of his community. In the West, however, we are still inclined to link giftedness with academic or scholastic performance to the detriment of the child with mechanical dexterity or the one who is incredibly streetwise!

A detailed study undertaken by Benjamin Bloom (1985) highlights the very real danger that the impression may be created that academic performance is the main indicator of giftedness, or that it is something you received as a gift and you may now rest on your laurels. Bloom identified 25 top achievers in six fields of study, under the age of 25 in the USA. After comprehensive discussions with all of these people, the following conclusions were reached:

- none of the individuals reached their level of giftedness within 12 years of schooling
- without exception they testified that their specific talents had been discovered at a very youthful age
- all testified to hard work and long hours of practice, even after they had reached the level of giftedness
- at an early age they had already learnt skills and subject matter that were later of the utmost importance in their specific fields.

Gifted is as gifted does

It is evident from Bloom's study and what has already been discussed, that hard work is required for reaching a level of giftedness, and that this hard work has to be maintained in order to continue to be recognized as achievement. One has a gift if one is gifted or talented; one ought to use that ability for oneself but also to work hard and use it for the good of society. A person should, perhaps, first provide proof of exceptional achievement before he or she may be called a gifted person. It is not the possession of a gift but the use to which it has been put, that would justify the claim of giftedness.

Unless a child's aptitudes and abilities are known and carefully assessed, he or she cannot possibly receive – except quite fortuitously – the programme of work, pace and degree of challenge he or she needs. If our gifted children are to receive social justice within our school system, we owe it to them to identify them and to adapt the curriculum to suit their needs.

It is important that a close relationship exists between the concept of giftedness, the characteristics of gifted and talented children, identification and programmes of learning for them. Increasingly, identification should be viewed as a part of good teaching: a continuous process that anticipates further challenging learning experiences with a quality end product. Seen that way, identification is an evaluation process that teachers undertake in the classroom, rather than a series of tests. Achievement tests are good indicators of specific academic talent; however, they usually have relatively low ceilings and they may not discriminate among gifted students who top out. Some teachers are still averse to standardized tests as one of the means of identifying gifted children, but the standardized attainment tests proposed by the government have their place, even though they are only one of many methods of identifying these children. Standardized tests may identify underachieving students – those whose grades and performance give no hint of the students' unused potential. Test scores are influenced by many factors, and so a low atypical response in a test should be verified against the student's other evidence of achievement, and if it still appears atypical, should be discarded. However, a high atypical response deserves further investigation. Is a child constantly in trouble, or a girl underachieving for social acceptance? Does the child have a specific learning disability, or emotional problems that make it difficult to learn and so disguise the student's gifts?

Teacher nomination in all aspects of the curriculum is to be recommended. Personality differences and busy classrooms mean that some children, however, may be overlooked or are not appreciated: for example, those with low motivation or underachieving children. Teachers, as we have seen, are not always the most accurate judges, and their observations need to be supplemented by other sources. Teachers are also wary of using parent nomination. Parents have lived with their children for five years before they come to school, so much has been laid down in the brain. I wonder how many schools still do not ask parents whether their pre-school child can read or write, or add or subtract. And, when children move into the secondary phase of education, how many colleagues there take cognisance of what has gone on in a child's education for the past 11 years?

Peer nomination and self-nomination are two other means of identification. The children know their classmates: ask any class who is the best in this class at mathematics, for example. They know each other well and know who is the first to finish, who gets their work right, and who to ask to help with their homework. They also know about the hidden curricula, and what a child does after school in their spare time. There is a good correlation between self- and peer nomination, so, why not use self-nomination as well?

Creativity tests may identify creative talent that is otherwise not visible. Because creativity is so complex, tests can only have moderate validity coefficients; creativity nevertheless is an important talent we need to identify, even though many of these children exhibit non-conformist behaviour in a classroom.

Identification should be ongoing, and the sooner it is started the more

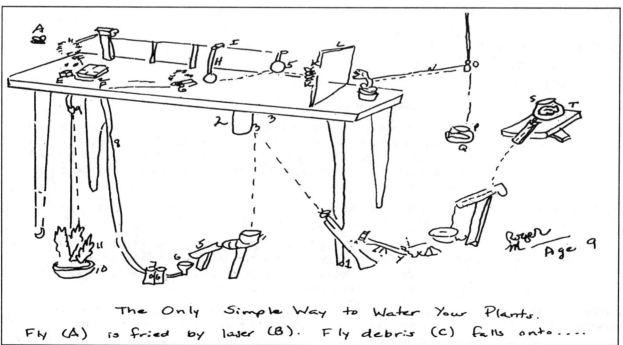

The Only Simple Way to Water Your Plants.
Fly (A) is fried by laser (B). Fly debris (C) falls onto....

Figure 2.5 *What do you do with your pot plants whilst on holiday? A problem? This is Roger's unique solution to this open-ended question*

advantageous it is for the child. However, identifying the gifted is far from being an exact science and we should err on the side of inclusion. It is suggested that we create a wide talent pool so that we can assess childrens' performance in enrichment activities (see Chapter 5). Teaching methods that emphasize problem solving, thinking skills and divergent responses, should provide the enrichment we need to nurture the strengths of children so that no child who has the potential to succeed is denied the opportunity of being identified and therefore extended. (See Roger's work, in Figure 2.5, for an example of divergent thinking.)

It is because of this important point that a close relationship should exist between the concept of giftedness, characteristics of gifted and talented children, identification and programmes of learning for them. Increasingly, identification should be viewed as a part of good teaching, a continuous process that anticipates further challenging learning experiences with a quality end product. In that way, identification is an evaluation process that teachers undertake in the classroom rather than being a series of tests. No identification is perfect, but to do nothing is an active choice and is a decision to ignore one section of the student population. Criteria, yes, must be defensible, yet objective criteria should be modified by subjective concern for children. Every child is entitled to the best programme, the most attentive care and the greatest love and respect that we can conceive and provide.

Our aim, then, as teachers, is to create a didactic and administratively flexible structure within which schools can design a programme according to the needs of these children within a broad framework. Pupils may then have the competence to fulfil their role in society with integrity and joy, as enterprising, independent, creative and productive members, in order to fulfil their considerable potential and realize their aspirations.

Summary of methods used for assessing high ability

Method	Use and limitations
Teacher observation	This is essential; the trained teacher should know his/her children but may miss those who do not conform to accepted standards of work or behaviour; children who present motivational or emotional problems, with belligerent or apathetic attitudes; children who come from homes that do not share the school's ethos.
Checklists and rating scales	Useful as a guide to what to look out for; may not be relevant for individual cases. Quick and easy to administer.
Intelligence tests	These group tests can be useful as an *initial* screen to supplement and counterbalance teacher observations. May not identify those with motivational or emotional problems, those with reading difficulties, or those from different ethnic/cultural backgrounds.
Achievement test batteries	Helpful in providing more detailed information on a wider range of skills, subject to same limitations as group tests. Will not necessarily identify the true abilities of children, nor leadership or social skills.
Creativity tests	May offer a chance to show quality of imagination and divergent thinking in

those overlooked by conventional tests above. Difficult area to define, assess and measure accurately.

Individual intelligence tests

Provide more accurate and reliable information on ability to 'reason' in conventional terms. May not indicate how a child will perform in class, nor predict achievement in individual cases. Costly in use of time, and subject to cultural bias.

Creative learning environments

This is the all-important ingredient, encouraging all children to explore their talents, exercise their developing capacity to learn and understand, and to reach the highest potential of which they are capable.

Nomination

Useful information from peer group, parents and child to build up a profile.

Figure 2.6 *Multiple approach to the identification of the gifted and talented*

One school with a keen special needs coordinator uses a simple chart like the one shown in Figure 2.7 to identify children with problems but also potential. This is followed by an action plan. The children discussed in this book often have special needs (see George, 1992; Leydon, 1990).

Name_____Date of Birth _____
School_____Year _____
Objective _____

_____

	WHAT?	HOW, WITH WHOM?	BY WHEN?	LIKELY PROBLEMS	POSSIBLE SOLUTIONS
STAGE 1					
STAGE 2					
STAGE 3					

SPECIAL NEEDS
CLASS

Rel. — Religion   L.D. – Learning Difficulties
E/B — Emotional Behavioural   SS — Social Services   A – Agencies

Name _____

D.O.B. _____

S.11. _____

E.S.L. _____

Rel. _____

L.D. _____

E/B _____

Medical _____

Diet _____

SS A _____

Bright _____

Gifted Learner _____

Under Achiever _____

Figure 2.7 *Action plan*

CHAPTER 3

Brain, Mind and Thinking

Something I owe to the soil that grew,
More to the life that fed.
But most to Allah, who gave me two
Separate sides to my head.
                    (Rudyard Kipling)

We take it for granted that our mind is in some way linked with our brain, and if it resides anywhere it must be somewhere in our head. In fact, this is a relatively recent notion, for the Egyptians believed that mind/spirit/soul resided not in the brain but in the bowels and heart, and Aristotle saw the heart as a seat of thought and feeling. For how can we study the mind when we use the mind to study it? This problem has taxed philosophers, thinkers and theologians throughout the ages, and the study of the mind in reality encompasses the study of mankind. In this short chapter we can only give an overview of a very complex subject, relating it particularly to our most able children.

In most definitions of giftedness, a high level of intelligence is viewed as advanced and accelerated brain function. The fabric of the brain is set down as a result of the interaction of genetic blueprints and environmental influences. Throughout this book the emphasis has been on the education of the whole child thinking positively.

One way of judging how highly evolved an animal is, for example, is by looking at how complex a nervous system it has. The most primitive animals have a very simple nervous system and network of nerve fibres running throughout their bodies. However, more advanced animals need to be able to react to different kinds of environments and stimuli; their nervous system is more complex, and has developed special structures to control different forms of behaviour and activity. In order to study the nervous system, we need to know exactly how it works, how a message travels up a nerve for instance, and what different kinds of nerve cells there are. This basic information was probably studied by teachers at university, but the plea here is that we should be aware of recent developments in brain science as it is an area with serious implications for education.

The human brain begins to develop about three weeks after conception, with thousands of new cells developing each minute. It is understandable now why doctors advise parents-to-be to go into training four months before conception, as they can improve the quality and potentiality of their child-to-be. The adult brain weighs approximately three pounds, and a second pound is added during the first year after birth, mostly in the cerebellum. The third pound develops between the ages of 2 and 16. Most experts would say that something like 90 per cent of the brain cells are laid down by weight before a child is 5; this gives credence to the argument that the early years, when so much information is taken in through the senses to the brain, are the most important.

The brain weighs 2 per cent of an adult's bodyweight and uses 20 per cent of all the body's energy. The brain generates something like 25 watts of energy when a person is awake, and not much less when they sleep. Information travels through the brain at something like 250 miles an hour, a tremendous amount of information passing through the corpus callosum. The cortex makes up 85 per cent of the brain mass and acts on the basis of the models and problem-solving techniques it develops. The process of learning can be enhanced by increasing the strengths and speed of transmission of synaptic activity; through changes in teaching styles and learning procedures, the growth of dendrite branching can be increased. These are the measurable differences in brains that show advances and accelerated development. It seems to me that at birth nearly everyone is programmed to be outstanding. By the environment we provide, we change not just the behaviour of children but we change them at the cellular level. In this way gifted children become different from average learners, not at birth but as a result of using and developing the complex structure they were born with.

Barbara Clarke (1988) uses a delightful analogy to help us understand the basic structure and function of the brain. If you make a fist with each of your hands so that you see the fingernails, and then place your hands together with the fingernails touching, as you look down at your hands they now form a very respectable model of the human brain. Move your little fingers and you have identified the area through which vision enters the brain. Move your middle fingers and you have located the motor area. The language area is just below the middle knuckle on the right hand (left hemisphere), though please note that it is connected to the right hemisphere (left hand) by way of the touching fingernails which now represent the corpus callosum. This connection between the right and left hemisphere of the brain has within it more neuroconnections than there are in any other part of the body.

The major part of the brain is made up of two hemispheres joined by millions of neurons. The left hemisphere controls the movement on the right side of the body, and the right hemisphere controls the left side of the body. In addition, the left hemisphere governs those functions principally to do with speech, rational thought, logical reasoning and objective analysis, while the right hemisphere is concerned with how things relate to one another. The right hemisphere recognizes shapes, patterns and images, and it covers our intuitive sense. It appears that each hemisphere can function independently of the other and that in most people one hemisphere plays a more dominant role. For most people, the left hemisphere is the dominant one, resulting in more right-handed people (90 per cent of the population). Not only does the dominant hemisphere govern the movement and handedness, but it seems to determine the prevailing consciousness or mode of thought. We have the capacity for two modes of mental functioning, each governed by a different part of our brain. Part of the conflict we experience inside ourselves in our daily lives is an extension of the conflict that occurs between the functioning of the two hemispheres. How often have we heard people say, 'I am in two minds about that'? It is comparatively recently that we have begun to understand the working of the mind from this perspective and it has allowed many individuals to become aware of the potential not only in the less dominant hemisphere (usually the right) but in the wisdom that arises when both hemispheres operate not in conflict but in harmony. Creating this balance in our mental life may require us to increase the functioning of our less dominant hemisphere and then balance the activity from each side. A good analogy is that of a stereo system where the stereo effect is greater than the sum of the two speakers.

From this brief section and by studying Figure 3.1, one can see that the educational system, particularly the National Curriculum, is biased towards left brain activities. One would make a plea for keeping a fair balance which should include music, art and drama, and physical education, which are subjects for life and living, and not just for jobs.

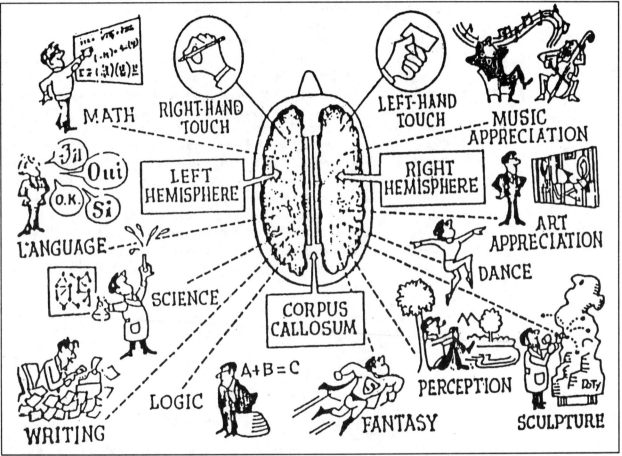

Figure 3.1   *How the brain divides its work*

Let us consider language in a little more detail as just one essential part of a child's education and one which distinguishes us from other animals. The whole question of how and how much the right hemisphere can acquire limited language skills is currently being debated. The right hemisphere's capacity to learn language can be triggered by early injury to the left brain. There are even a few examples of active language development in both hemispheres. If this is so, is it possible that right brain linguistic sensitivity could be brought about by a person's having to undergo some form of untraumatic pressure such as sustained curiosity? The typical right brain not only deals with manipulative and spatial actions, but also appears to have a gift, which contrasts with the left hemisphere's analytical powers, for offering holistic and synthetic solutions to problems. When confronted with difficulties or problems, each hemisphere appears to show a capacity for helping the other. They are not competitive and it would seem probable that this readiness to cooperate with and to defer to the other side may be an important variable – one which could be greatly affected by our educational system. This might explain what is commonly referred to as the difference between convergent and divergent thinking (see Figure 3.1).

In the normal situation of active learning, airing of the two cerebral viewpoints will produce a constant, largely unconscious, dialectic. For example, try naming a scientific problem which worries you, even saying it out loud, then, using your right hemisphere intuitive capabilities, build up a picture. In any such work the right hemisphere seems to prefer not to be hurried. This means that problems need to be given time in order that concrete operations processing may proceed at leisure.

We can now begin to see why learning by doing can justify its claims to be at the very heart of genuine education. Such doing may be unspectacular and invisible to an observer, but it is the essential condition for full brain consultation. Teachers' presentation of a cue or a diagram is often of great importance, but it is the learner acting on it that brings about the acquisition of a new concept. The mind, which means all the parts working in concert, generally acts as a totality which is committed at conscious and unconscious levels to making sense of what is going on. This means that a good way of understanding your mind is to examine what it produces and how these products themselves affect the working of the mind. The first product of the mind that we have already alluded to in this book is the capacity for awareness, curiosity and consciousness. Space does not allow us to go further along this direction, but the following list shows suggested products of the mind which, together with the chart showing influences on the mind, are vitally important:

Products of the mind	Influences on the mind
Knowledge	Climate
Dreams	Ions
Fantasies	Food
Thoughts	Drugs
Feelings	Society
Image	Culture
Ideas	Families
Consciousness	Health
Language	
	– to name but a few –

To take one example, numerous additives that are now present in many of our food substances make certain children hyperactive and certainly deny their potential for mood change. Another example is social, cultural and racial factors as external influences on the mind. These differences often surface in the language of each nationality. For example, Eskimos have over seven different words for snow; in their environment the necessity to differentiate between one form of snow and another is much more important than it is for an English person. Because we have no other word for snow than 'snow', we can only think of snow in one way. It has been said that words put chains on thoughts, and it is not difficult to see how our cultural and national inheritance both shapes and limits our capacity for awareness.

There is the possible danger when we think about learning and education and about the physiological structures on which they depend, that we make a thing or machine out of the learner, or we lapse inadvertently into what Oscar Wilde once called 'Stuffing stuff into kids'. It would be all too easy to take an instrumental approach to education, reacting to calls to concentrate on 'values' and 'facts'. In this age of the rapid expansion of knowledge, facts are like fish – they sometimes go off! If any reader has doubts about the potentialities of their right hemisphere, they might find it worth reading through Betty Edwards' book, *Drawing on the Right Side of the Brain* (1992); it is remarkable and revealing as well as being a therapeutic experience.

Not only is there a constant or creative middle way to be sought between the two main kinds of cerebral process, but we must also assume that similar integration goes on between these and other brain systems and between all these and the neuromuscular and endocrine activities which underlie them. They all affect our moods, our health, our energy and our direction. The different parts of our brain and their functions must not be seen as being in opposition; the hemispheres are complementary, interactive, and by working simultaneously enable us to cope with complex tasks. For both parents and teachers it is our duty to be aware of the rapidly growing area of brain science and research. One fascinating example is provided by Ned Herrmann in the United States. His concept of whole brain teaching and learning is based upon a distribution of specialized modes throughout the brain system. He has developed a model that divides the brain into four separate quadrants, each one different and equal in importance. Two of these quadrants represent the more cognitive intellectual modes associated with the two cerebral hemispheres. The other two quadrants represent the more visceral, emotional modes associated with the limbic system. Two of the four quadrants are specialized in left mode thinking processes. These are the more logical, analytical, quantitative and fact-based modes contained in the cerebral left quadrant, and the more planned, organized, detailed and sequential mode processed in the limbic left quadrant. In contrast, the other two quadrants make up right mode specialization. These include the more synthesizing, integrating, holistic and intuitive modes associated with the cerebral right quadrant, and the interpersonal, emotional kinesthetic and feeling modes associated with the right limbic quadrant. If this research continues and proves to be true, then it has serious implications for education. Figure 3.2 gives just an example of Herrmann's current thinking and his book, *The Creative Brain* (1986), is a challenging read with its implications for learning styles correlated to modes of the brain and our approach to delivering the curriculum.

Whole brain teaching and learning

Learning is mental.
The learner's brain is unique and specialized.
The brain is situational.
Unique individuals have different learning styles.
Learning designs can accommodate individual differences.
Delivery of learning can respond to personal uniqueness.
Unique people can be made an integral part of the learning design.
Learners can be grouped in schools to make the learning more effective.
Learning through affirmation and discovery can be more effective, fulfilling, enjoyable and longer-lasting.

The following exhibit shows the differences in the learning styles represented by the specialized modes of each of the four quadrants

LEARNING STYLES REPRESENTED BY THE
SPECIALIZED MODES OF THE FOUR QUADRANTS

A Upper Left	D Upper Right
<u>LEARNS BY:</u> ACQUIRING AND QUANTIFYING FACTS APPLYING ANALYSIS AND LOGIC THINKING THROUGH IDEAS BUILDING CASES FORMING THEORIES	<u>LEARNS BY:</u> TAKING INITIATIVE EXPLORING HIDDEN POSSIBILITIES RELYING ON INTUITION SELF DISCOVERY CONSTRUCTING CONCEPTS SYNTHESIZING CONTENT
B Lower Left	C Lower Right
<u>LEARNS BY:</u> ORGANIZING AND STRUCTURING CONTENT SEQUENCING CONTENT EVALUATING AND TESTING THEORIES ACQUIRING SKILLS THROUGH PRACTICE IMPLEMENTING COURSE CONTENT	<u>LEARNS BY:</u> LISTENING AND SHARING IDEAS INTEGRATING EXPERIENCES WITH SELF MOVING AND FEELING HARMONIZING WITH THE CONTENT EMOTIONAL INVOLVEMENT

Experience has shown that different design and delivery approaches facilitate learning in each of these four specialized quadrants. The following exhibit shows these four different design and delivery approaches.

DESIGN AND DELIVERY APPROACHES FOR THE
SPECIALIZED MODES OF THE FOUR QUADRANTS

A Upper Left	D Upper Right
<u>LEARNERS RESPOND TO:</u> FORMALIZED LECTURE DATA BASED CONTENT FINANCIAL/TECHNICAL CASE DISCUSSIONS TEXT BOOKS AND BIBLIOGRAPHIES PROGRAMME LEARNING BEHAVIOUR MODIFICATION	<u>LEARNERS RESPOND TO:</u> SPONTANEITY FREE FLOW EXPERIMENTAL OPPORTUNITIES EXPERIMENTATION PLAYFULNESS FUTURE ORIENTED CASE DISCUSSIONS VISUAL DISPLAYS AESTHETICS INDIVIDUALITY BEING INVOLVED
B Lower Left	C Lower Right
<u>LEARNERS RESPOND TO:</u> THOROUGH PLANNING STRUCTURE SEQUENTIAL ORDER LECTURES ORGANIZATIONAL AND ADMINISTRATIVE CASE STUDIES TEXT BOOKS PROGRAMME LEARNING BEHAVIOUR MODIFICATION	<u>LEARNERS RESPOND TO:</u> EXPERIENTIAL OPPORTUNITIES SENSORY MOVEMENT MUSIC PEOPLE ORIENTED CASE DISCUSSIONS GROUP INTERACTION

© NED HERRMANN (1986) *The Creative Brain*

Figure 3.2   *Teaching and learning*

This leads naturally to encouraging children to think, which is what education hopefully is largely about. However, cognitive development is so often taught to the detriment of the other talent areas we have already discussed. It is generally acknowledged that far too much classroom learning is concerned with traditional academic knowledge and routine skills, rather than teaching children to think, reason and solve problems in a creative way. Thinking skills can be strengthened and improved through exercises in a similar way to a sports practices. Creative thinking may be taught directly by helping students to understand creative people and creative processes. Critical thinking may be taught by teaching children to observe and look critically at opinion or newspaper articles. Examples of Bloom's taxonomy are discussed in Chapter 5, and much of the work in teaching thinking skills has recognized his impact on this area. His taxonomy describes progressively higher levels of cognitive activity. This encouragement to think is commonly called metacognition, that is, thinking about thinking, and students should understand their thinking strategies and why and when these strategies may be used. These strategies include the following:

- challenging existing ways of doing things as a means of stimulating new ideas
- strengthening the intellectual abilities through practice and exercise
- decision making which requires considering the factors involved and possible alternatives
- perhaps we should be concentrating on problem finding rather than problem solving. Do we ever ask the children what the problems of our school and of our society are? They often have incredible ideas that we may not even have thought of. For example, what do we do on a wet playtime in school? How do we prevent litter being dropped in school, let alone problems of the world such as the population explosion and pollution.

Following are a few examples of issues to present to our gifted children to encourage them to think:

1. If you could run a school any way you wanted to run it, what would you do? Who would go to your school? Who could teach at it? Would there be classes to attend? How and for how long would students go to school? Would you have any rules about how students would have to behave in your school? Would you have any rules about what students could wear to your school? Would there be any lower or upper age limit for your students? Would there be any lower or upper age limit for teachers? What kinds of general rules would you have for your school? What would you do about someone who did not obey the rules? Who would pay for the cost of running your school?

2. Traffic accidents result in great losses of life and property every year. Suppose you were a dictator with absolute power to enforce your demands. What would you do to decrease the number of traffic accidents?

3. Suppose you were born a hundred years from now. How would your life be different from what it is now?

4. More and more medical scientists are finding cures for different types of cancer. But it still seems that cancer is killing many more people than it did, say, 50 years ago. Why do you suppose this is so?

5. Figure 3.3 shows four different newspaper reports of the same accident. A

A FACTS	C FUTURES
"Once again...forensic science using the undeniable facts of blood type, fingerprints, and spectrographic analysis of paint fragments prove beyond doubt..."	"This accident demonstrates the lethal combination of drunk driving and faulty car design. These two issues are national in scope and deserve urgent Congressional attention if future generations are to be adequately protected..."
"At 1:15 am, Thursday, April 9th, on Route 9, 15 miles north of Columbus a black, 1978 Plymouth, 4-door sedan travelling at 75 miles per hour in a 35 mph school zone..." **B FORM**	"Tearful, screaming mother attacks the cowering suspect as irate police officers hold off an angry mob at the terrifying scene of a tangled school bus and the accident's bloody victims...." **D FEELINGS**

Figure 3.3 *Four reporters' accounts of the same accident*

good exercise to do with gifted children is to discuss these in relation to the four quarters of the brain.

6. Suppose everyone in the world was exactly like everyone else. Could some people have different jobs than others? Could some people speak different languages than other people? Could some people live in different countries than other people? Could some people have different ideas than other people? Do you think people would be happier than they are now, or not? Would your answer to the above vary according to what everyone was like? Would it matter whether everyone was a liar and a thief or an extremely honest person? Would it matter whether everyone was dull-witted or very intelligent? What other things would matter, do you think?

1. To give students experiences of thinking skills they have not previously experienced.
2. To teach vocabulary concepts operations and relationships necessary for problem solving.
3. To translate the abstract thinking into everyday examples which the student can relate to.
4. To increase motivation.
5. To encourage reflective thinking.
6. To use lateral thinking.
7. To raise students' expectations of themselves as thinkers and learners.
8. To raise self-esteem and give students the confidence to take risks.

Table 3.1 *Goals for thinking skills*

The worksheet in Figure 3.4 gives further examples which the author has worked with children; they found them to be most thought-provoking but also enjoyable. These exercises of creative learning can result in improved motivation, achievement, creativity, self-confidence, and better attitudes towards school and others. The exercises include exploring, questioning, experimenting, testing ideas and other activities. This form of creative learning includes sensing a problem, formulating hypotheses or guesses, testing, revising, and retesting these hypotheses, as well as communicating results to others.

CREATIVE THINKING

Creative thinking is simply about coming up with unusual solutions to different questions and problems. Here is a list of situations. See if you can think of a novel way of tackling each one.

If you were King of the Castle, what would you do if your serfs went on strike?

Five new planets have just been discovered. Think of different names for each of them. Give reasons why you have chosen the names.

Make five new laws of the land and give reasons why you have made them.

List all the qualities you look for in a friend. Which is the most important, and why?

Describe what a television set sees as it sits and watches you.

With the invention of CDs, vinyl records have become obsolete. List all the things you could do with your old record collection.

Figure 3.4   *From George (1994)*

CHAPTER 4

Multiple Intelligences

*There is no meaning to life except the meaning man gives his life
by the unfolding of his powers.*

(Eric Fromm)

As has been indicated, there exists an extensive history of approaches to the
identification of gifted and talented individuals. One of the most widely
implemented methods has been the administration of a standardized measure
of intelligence – the 'IQ Test'. Many hundreds of tests have been devised to
measure individuals' capabilities and readiness for a range of academic and
professional situations. The testing industry has become an increasingly
powerful decision maker in our society, and there are concerns that such tests
may determine people's life-chances. Many, if not most, of these tests rely
heavily on the test taker's performance on a series of rapid-fire, short answer or
multiple choice questions based largely on the linguistic and mathematical areas
of a person's talents. What results is a snapshot of the individual's capabilities
at a precise point in time under an often stressful situation in a limited range of
intellectual abilities. The testing community has had a particularly strong
impact on the identification of the children we are discussing in this book.

Today, however, we talk about multiple intelligences, whereby it is now
recognized that many children have individual talents, apart from being broadly
gifted. In 1983 Howard Gardner wrote a fascinating book entitled *Frames of
Mind,* in which he challenges the notion of a general intelligence, or G, on
which most models of intelligence testing had so far been based. He questions
the idea that individuals' intellectual capabilities can be captured in a single
measure of intelligence, and as the term 'multiple intelligences' suggests, he
believes that human cognitive competence is better described as a set of
abilities, talents, or mental skills that he has chosen to call intelligences. He
defines intelligence as an ability or set of abilities that permit an individual to
solve problems or fashion products that are of consequence in a particular
cultural setting. Gardner's research for this work was drawn from several
sources, including development in normal and gifted individuals; the
breakdown of skills under conditions of brain damage; autistic children;
psychometric studies; and studies on the training of particular skills.

We now realize there is a need for a better classification of human intellectual
competences, because there is much recent evidence emerging from scientific
research, cross-cultural observations and educational studies, which stands in

need of review and organization and perhaps, above all, because it seems within our grasp to come up with a list of intellectual strengths which should prove useful to both researchers and practitioners in the future. Others are now following this line of research as we learn more and more from brain science, and the reader is recommended to the work of Ned Herrmann (1986) in his book *The Creative Brain* (see Figure 3.2).

Talents seem to emerge from general ability as the coming together of genetic dispositions coupled with the home and school experiences as well as a child's unique interest and learning styles. Genetic factors are seen as determining potential strengths and setting limits to the extent of talent development. Those children who are likely to go on to high level talent development will exhibit precocity early on, and aptitudes, abilities and intelligences emerge as a result of experiences, motivations and learning styles. There is an increasing interest in individual talent development as apart from the few children who are broadly gifted. 'Talent development is the business of our field, and we must never lose sight of this goal, regardless of the direction that reform efforts may take' (Renzulli, 1991). Renzulli's work, along with that of Gardner (op cit) and Feldhusen (1994), sets the stage for a major reconceptualization of gifted education. This broad review helped to include the under-served populations in this movement, as it is certainly clear that some minority, economically disadvantaged and culturally different populations are not often included in providing for these children. This comparatively new concept of talent or special intelligences suggests a more analytical and more diverse view of human abilities, abilities which may be nurtured to full development.

Some children show talent or specific aptitudes in mathematics, some in verbal communication or other talent areas very early on in school; others will exhibit their talents later. There is a wide difference between young people in both their aptitudes for different areas, and in their interest or motivation in pursuing their studies. Home and community influences seem to foster growth of these talents, and nature and nurture operate simultaneously in a school. It is now considered that giftedness is a static concept, whereas talents is a dynamic concept in which individual children can grow and develop with the right nurturing. The author has met children who can read at 3 with a vocabulary of 500 words, and children who learn calculus in the junior department; he has also met children who have been turned off school simply because they were not challenged early on.

Feldhusen and others have presented evidence from research of talents showing themselves in vocational areas such as agriculture, business, and home economics. In addition, these young people show characteristics including skills in designing and conducting projects, superior problem-solving ability, and resourcefulness in finding information.

Gardner's intelligences might best be seen as an early more general form of ability, probably highly genetically determined, that fine focuses later in more specific vocations, as shown in the talent development chart in Figure 4.1. It also correlates well with Renzulli's rating scales of behavioural characteristics of these able young people. Essential, however, to the theory of multiple intelligences is the concept that each of the intelligences varies independently in individuals, and individuals show unique profiles of strengths and weaknesses among the seven intelligences. Gardner speaks of a giftedness matrix which can be a combination of one, two or more intelligences.

Definitions of the seven intelligences

Gardner (1983) lists seven intelligences. Every normal person possesses a unique blend of all these intelligences; talented children tend to be advanced in one area:

1. Verbal/linguistic
2. Musical/rhythmic
3. Logical/mathematical
4. Visual/spatial
4. Body/kinesthetic
6. Intrapersonal
7. Interpersonal

Verbal/Linguistic Intelligence

Verbal/linguistic intelligence is the ability to use with clarity the core operations of language. People with verbal/linguistic intelligence have a sensitivity to the meaning of words – the capacity to follow rules of grammar and, on carefully selected occasions, to violate them. At a somewhat more sensory level, they have a sensitivity to the sounds, rhythms, inflections and meters of words – that ability which can make even poetry in a foreign tongue beautiful to hear. They also have sensitivity to the different functions of language – its potential to excite, convince, stimulate, convey information, or simply to please. Poets, authors, reporters, public speakers, solicitors, talk-show hosts and politicians may exhibit linguistic intelligence.

Musical/Rhythmic Intelligence

Musical/rhythmic intelligence is the ability to use the core set of musical elements – pitch, rhythm and timbre, and the characteristic qualities of a tone. For example, Leonard Bernstein had lots of it; Mozart, presumably, had even more. As with any intelligence, it is displayed in various degrees of intensity, from the avant-garde composer attempting to create music, to the fledgling listener who is trying to make sense of nursery rhymes. There may well be a hierarchy of difficulty involved in various roles, with performing exacting more demands than listening does, and composing making more profound – or at least different – demands than performing. Musical ability is hard to define or pin down. It has its roots in emotion, affect and pleasure. As Roger Sessions put it, 'music is controlled movement of sound and time...It is made by humans who want it, enjoy it, and even love it.' Musical intelligence may be demonstrated by singers, composers, instrumentalists, conductors, and by those who enjoy, understand, or appreciate music.

Logical/Mathematical Intelligence

Logical/mathematical intelligence is logical and mathematical ability as well as scientific ability. What characterizes individuals with high logical/mathematical intelligence is a love for abstraction. Mathematicians must be absolutely rigorous and perennially sceptical: no fact can be accepted unless it has been proved rigorously by steps that are derived from universally accepted first principles. They must skilfully handle long chains of reasoning and be able to recognize significant problems and solve them. While science and mathematics are closely allied, they can be clearly distinguished. While mathematicians are interested in exploring abstract systems for their own sake, scientists are motivated by a desire to explain physical reality. For the scientist, mathematics are a tool for building models and theories that can describe and, eventually, explain the operation of the world. Mathematicians, engineers, physicists, astronomers, researchers may demonstrate logical/mathemical intelligence.

Visual/Spatial Intelligence

Spatial intelligence is the capacity to perceive the visual world accurately and to be able to recreate one's visual experience. It entails a number of loosely related capacities: the ability to recognize instances of the same element; the ability to recognize transformations of one element in another; the capacity to conjure up mental imagery and then to transform that imagery; the ability to produce a graphic likeness of spatial information, and the like. A person with a good sense of direction or the ability to maneouvre and operate well in the world would have a high degree of spatial intelligence, as well as someone who worked with graphic depictions of the spatial world, such as maps, diagrams, paintings or sculptures. Navigators, engineers, surgeons, sculptors and painters all have highly developed spatial intelligence, as well as cartographers and architects.

Body/Kinesthetic Intelligence

Bodily/kinesthetic intelligence is the control of one's bodily motions and the ability to handle objects skilfully. Those possessing high levels of bodily/kinesthetic intelligence utilize their bodies or parts of their bodies as a means to fashion products, solve problems, or express themselves. Actors, dancers, swimmers, acrobats, for example, develop keen mastery over the motions of their bodies, as well as those individuals like artisans, ball players and jugglers who are able to manipulate objects with finesse.

Intrapersonal Intelligence

Intrapersonal intelligence is the ability to form an accurate model of oneself, and to use that model to operate effectively in life. Intrapersonal intelligence is, at its most basic level, the capacity to distinguish a feeling of pleasure from one of emotional pain and, on the basis of such discrimination, to become more involved or to withdraw from a situation. At its most advanced level, intrapersonal intelligence is the capacity to detect and to symbolize complex and highly differentiated sets of feelings. One finds this intelligence developed in the novelist who can write introspectively about feelings, in the patient or therapist who comes to attain a deep knowledge of his or her own feeling life; in the wise elder who draws upon his or her own wealth of inner experience in order to advise members of his or her community; in psychologists and philosophers; in those who can be single-minded.

Interpersonal Intelligence

Interpersonal intelligence is the ability to notice and make distinctions among other individuals and, in particular, between their moods, temperaments, motivations and intentions. Interpersonal intelligence turns outward to other individuals. Examined in its most elementary form, the interpersonal intelligence entails the capacity of the young child to discriminate among the individuals around him or her and to detect their various moods. In an advanced form, interpersonal intelligence permits a skilled adult to read the intentions and desires – even when those desires have been hidden – of many other individuals and, potentially, to act upon this knowledge: for example, by influencing a group of individuals to behave along desired lines. We see highly developed forms of interpersonal intelligence in political or religious leaders (a Mahatma Gandhi or Lyndon Johnson), in skilled parents or teachers, and in individuals enrolled in the helping professions, such as therapists or counsellors, minsters of religion and teachers.

Colleagues may now like to put this theoretical model into practice and use the following as a checklist to find the strengths of individual children.

INTELLIGENCES CHECKLIST

Verbal/Linguistic intelligence. A capability in this area would show itself in those who can tell rich and coherent stories or report with accuracy on experiences they have had, not simply in the ability to repeat sentences and define words on the standard measure of intelligence.

Musical/rhythmic intelligence. Musical children can be seen singing to themselves as they tell a story; noticing the different sounds in their environment; and they have the ability to hear themes in music and good pitch discrimination.

Mathematical intelligence. This area represents the skills most addressed and valued in a traditional school setting; together with linguistic intelligence, it continues to form the basis of a great majority of standardized measures of intelligence, even though their prominence outside the school setting can be challenged.

Visual/spatial intelligence. In children a facility with puzzles or other spatial problem-solving activities are good indications, as is being good at designing objects.

Body/kinesthetic intelligence. A child with this ability can be seen moving expressively in response to different musical and verbal stimuli or demonstrating keen sporting ability in organized games or in the playground.

Intrapersonal. There are the children who have a keen knowledge and understanding of their own ability as well as a range of emotions. They get frustrated when the bell goes just when they are getting into something in great depth: they can be very single-minded about a topic they are working on.

Interpersonal. Children skilled in this area can be perceived as leaders and organizers in the classroom, knowing how and where other children spend their time; they are sensitive to the needs and feelings of others. These are the children who care for one another.

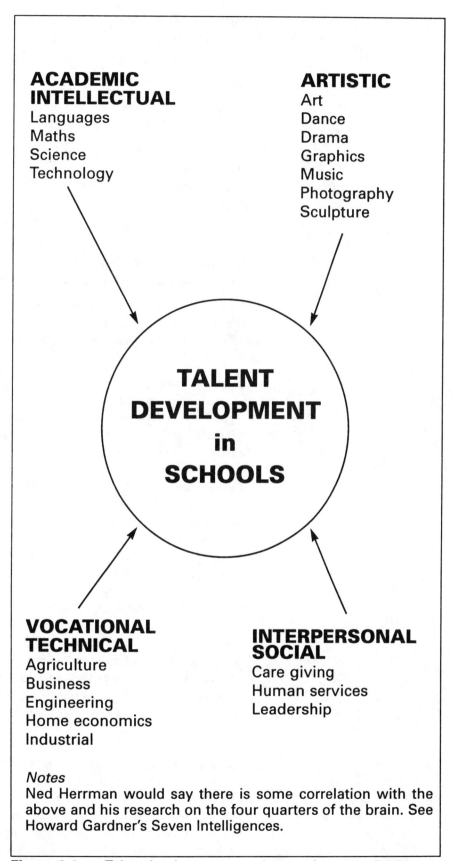

ACADEMIC INTELLECTUAL
Languages
Maths
Science
Technology

ARTISTIC
Art
Dance
Drama
Graphics
Music
Photography
Sculpture

TALENT DEVELOPMENT in SCHOOLS

VOCATIONAL TECHNICAL
Agriculture
Business
Engineering
Home economics
Industrial

INTERPERSONAL SOCIAL
Care giving
Human services
Leadership

Notes
Ned Herrman would say there is some correlation with the above and his research on the four quarters of the brain. See Howard Gardner's Seven Intelligences.

Figure 4.1 *Talent development* — Adapted from John Feldhusen

More recent is the concept of talent development set forth by Bloom (1985) in which he proposed four distinct areas of talent:

1. athletic or psycho-motor
2. aesthetic, musical and artistic
3. cognitive or intellectual
4. interpersonal relations.

From his intensive case studies of the lives of talented people, he concluded that talent potential is present in many children and can be facilitated by family and teachers. Early recognition and nurturance is vital, and motivation is a crucial ingredient. He concludes,

> All of this is to point to the enormous human potential available in each society and the likelihood that only a very small amount of this human potential is ever fully developed. We believe that each society could vastly increase the amount and kinds of talent it develops.

The author suggests that these four domains should not be viewed as encompassing all talents, as there are certainly many more. My own list of intelligences, based on many years of observation of children and young people, is as follows:

Linguistic intelligence – the one who speaks several languages and can pick up another within a month.

Analytical intelligence – the person who loves intellectual problems, crosswords and puzzles. Scientists and academics are strong in this type of intelligence and, especially when it is combined with factual intelligence, examinations come easy.

Factual intelligence – the sort of people who are walking encyclopaedias, who win the Mastermind competition and give impromptu factual talks.

Musical intelligence – the intelligence that gave Mozart his genius, but also drives young pop stars and their bands, many of whom never had a chance of going to university because their scores on the second and third intelligences described above would have been too low.

Spatial intelligence – which sees patterns in things. Artists have it, as do some systems designers and mathematicians.

Physical intelligence – the intelligence or talent which we can see in sports stars, which enables them to have tremendous eye/hand coordination or be able to hit a ball much further than others, or to dance better.

Practical intelligence – the intelligence which allows young people to take a car apart and put it back together again, though they may not be able to explain it in writing. Many so-called 'intellectuals' are notoriously impractical and often unworldly.

Intuitive intelligence – this is a talent which some have of seeing things which others cannot, even if they cannot explain why or wherefore. We talk about a 'woman's intuition'; perhaps men do not have as much intuition, which may explain why they often disparage it!

Interpersonal intelligence – this is the person who has the ability and wit to get things done in and through people, and gets on really well with them. This intelligence often does not go with analytical or factual intelligence. These charismatic people are a great asset, and without this form of intelligence great minds can be wasted.

There are probably more types of intelligence; the important point to note is that it has many faces, all of them useful, all of them potentially valuable. The author would go so far as to say that everyone has at least one intelligence from this list, and it is the duty of parents and teachers to discover which child has what, and then to develop them to the full. However, discovering your intelligences is one thing, applying them is another. We need to be able to organize ourselves and other people to do something about them: what Charles Handy (1994) refers to as the skills of conceptualizing, coordinating; and consolidating; these are the verbs of education as opposed to the nouns, the doing words, not the facts. We do not learn to use these verbs by sitting in rows in a classroom, but by practice. I am reminded of the old Chinese proverb 'If I hear I forget, if I see I remember, if I do then I know'.

There is no single model that will optimize a child's talent development. Schools need the resources to match the child's talents and provide the nurturance for continuing growth of those talents. This is why this author emphasizes the affective curriculum and the need for a partnership between schools and parents. Talented young people should increasingly be taught to recognize and understand their own talents. Therefore they need to find the nurturing resources and activities that will enable them to become independent in guiding their own talent development.

CHAPTER 5

Enriching the Curriculum

The human mind, overstretched to a new idea, never goes back to its original dimensions.

(Oliver Wendell Holmes)

In Britain the main way of providing for able children up to recently has been to enrich the curriculum where the children are without too much segregation as the philosophy has been that we should teach children in mixed ability classes. However, the author's recent experience is that mixed ability teaching has declined and in comprehensive schools setting now seems to be the norm.

There are many interpretations of the term 'enrichment', though there are some ideas most would agree with. This was recognized by Ogilvie (1973) when he stated that 'enrichment will mean different things to different people, and represents something of an amalgam in the minds of us all'. It is defined in the *DES Glossary* as, 'A general term for a change in the quality of work to a level much higher than that normally expected of a particular age group'. Enrichment materials purport to promote or support a higher level of thinking. Enrichment is the most commonly accepted strategy for teaching able children in schools in this country but unfortunately it can be a concept which is not understood. All students may benefit from enrichment activities, especially those who come from non-enriched backgrounds. The author defined enrichment for the Oxford Research Project (Denton and Postlethwaite, 1985) as follows:

1. Is a broadening and deepening of the learning experience.

2. Provides experiences and activities beyond the regular curriculum.

3. Develops the intellectual gifts and talents of the most able.

4. Stresses qualitative development of thinking skills rather than quantitative accumulation of facts.

5. Emphasizes the process of learning rather than content.

6. Can be horizontal, exploring bodies of knowledge that are not frequently touched upon in the school common core curriculum.

7. Can be vertical, developing the skill of quantitative thinking which implies a facility with subject matter and ability to understand basic principles and to make generalizations.

8. Generally these children should do less and learn more. For example, it is generally preferable for a pupil to find three possible solutions to a problem

than to solve three problems of a similar nature.

We now have to ask ourselves, is enrichment specifically suited to the more able child? Is it an extra one hour a week added-on to something else, or a withdrawal group for an hour or two every two weeks? Does this in fact do much good? It is no good if it is more of the same; our definition states that the activities should provide for a higher level of abstraction, more creative thinking and more definite content. Enrichment, well thought out and carefully implemented, is based on pre-planned goals, the development of research skills, and the extension of concepts. To be effective the enrichment programme has to set objectives, provide for the excitement of learning, and lead to more advanced thinking. All our enrichment activities should be planned and designed with the following objectives in mind:

- content beyond the National Curriculum
- exposure to a variety of subjects
- student-selected content
- high content complexity
- maximum achievement in basic skills
- creative thinking and problem solving
- motivation.

It seems logical to consider enrichment and differentiating work together, as the concept of enrichment leads directly to differentiation. Most teachers provide a measure of enrichment work by writing suitable worksheets, modifying texts and encouraging children to read widely. As seen above, however, the process of enrichment is more than a simple provision of more demanding materials. Enrichment is an activity which is a function of the teacher's flexibility, sensitivity to individual needs, a sense of timing, and a mastery of subject area.

The National Curriculum emphasizes that curricula for all children should have breadth and depth, as well as balance and relevance; this cannot be provided by the National Curriculum alone. We need to remind ourselves constantly that the National Curriculum is a foundation to be augmented by additional subjects, cross-curricular themes, dimensions and skills as well as extra-curricular activities. The vision for the more able child must be formulated within this framework, and enrichment programmes should draw on a broader conceptualization of the subjects. It is the author's experience that the children we are discussing here have the ability to go way beyond Level Ten, and therefore we need to be prepared for that fact.

It is likely that enrichment programmes associated with each attainment level will be developed from amplification, elaboration and extension of the programmes of study at the same level of attainment, rather than the next level of attainment. Enrichment programmes of various kinds should benefit all pupils, from the most to the least able.

A Model for Core Extension

All children are entitled to an enriching curriculum, but many can be extended in order to move on to higher-order thinking skills, concepts and attitudes. The model shown in Figure 5.1 is recommended for such work. All children need a common core curriculum, but much of what it contains is often known by the able child; by asking some questions or giving a short test, this can be confirmed by the teachers. Where this is the case, the curriculum can be compacted so that these children can move on to more advanced work which will challenge them.

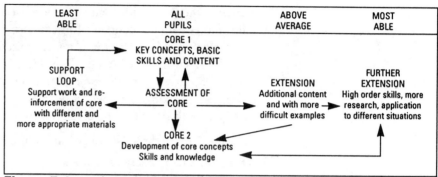

Figure 5.1   *A model for extension*

The Triad Enrichment Model advocated by Joe Renzulli (1977) in the United States has been modified to suit the British system of education by Wiltshire Local Education Authority, which advocates teachers planning a topic with their 'Must, Should and Could' grid; teachers on in-service courses have often produced excellent exemplars of this model in practice. (Figure 5.3 shows a completed grid based on a science topic on density.)

Examples of good practice

It is crucial that we match the curriculum to the demonstrated abilities of our children, and programmes for gifted and talented children should vary with the age level of the participants as well as the students' interests and needs. This section will explain two recommended models for differentiating the curriculum, and will refer to other models which are well worth considering.

Bloom's Taxonomy

Benjamin Bloom (1956) produced a series of cognitive levels that move from the simple to complex, to help teachers understand levels of learning and their interrelatedness. If busy teachers use these levels, they can design effective curriculum and evaluation activities across subject areas for all students. The taxonomy consists of six levels of thinking, starting with a knowledge base which will include remembering facts and information. The next level is comprehension, whereby a child will understand these facts.

Third is application, whereby one would expect a child to use the information and facts provided. Fourth is analysis: explaining information. Fifth is synthesis: creating something new by using information, and finally there is evaluation, whereby a child makes judgements based on the above criteria.

It is obvious that the first three levels are very basic for all students; the last three are critical in developing higher order thinking skills for our most able. If children have the opportunity to work on a differentiated worksheet, examples of which follow, then a teacher would be able to determine quite readily by asking questions or giving a test, at what level in the taxonomy a child is both confident and competent to work. The idea is to raise questions containing specific thinking levels, specific verbs which direct student thinking and action. Student outcomes become more complex as they progress up the thinking levels. The tasks at the top levels incorporate critical, creative, logical thinking and problem-solving activities. The following two worksheets give examples at different levels, and mainly consist of process verbs and products. The second model, which is warmly recommended, is based on the original triad enrichment model of Joe Renzulli in the United States, and has been adapted for use in Britain by Wiltshire LEA.

This model was developed originally to allow students the opportunity to pursue their own interests to whatever depth they are able. Children are encouraged to become active producers of new knowledge, and the role of the teacher is to help children to identify and frame the problem to be studied. There is an introductory activity followed by skills training activities that are good for all students, but when an able child has an interest and a desire to explore a topic further, an extended investigation is provided by the next level of the model. This model does, however, assume that there are differentiated resource banks available in schools, including good library facilities, and experts within the school or community to support this more detailed study. This model works particularly well when students are self-motivated and like challenges. The difficulty occurs when the task commitment is low. There follows the adaptation of this model which is recommended for teachers in planning any new topic at any age level. By law the National Curriculum states that teachers have to teach concepts, knowledge, skills and attitudes, which can be seen on the grid in Figure 5.2. The idea in planning a topic is that all children must have a common core curriculum but some can and should go further. Some children are able to go into much greater depth with higher order thinking skills, and (this is the final set of boxes in the grid) should be enabled to do so.

	MUST	SHOULD	COULD
Knowledge			
Concept			
Skills			
Attributes			

Figure 5.2   *Attitudes*

Following this grid there is a sample from science based on a topic on density, kindly contributed by a teacher who has attended one of the author's differentiation days (see Figure 5.3).

Other models worth investigating are the Bett's Autonomous Learner Model, Clarke's Integrated Educational Model, and the William's model for implementing cognitive/affective behaviour in the classroom (for further details see George, 1993).

C. Density + Sc1 Investigation			Year 7 Water
	MUST	SHOULD	COULD
CONCEPTS	Appreciate floating and sinking are related to shape and how heavy something is	Some things float because there is a balance in forces	Apply to living things (eg fish) and submarines
KNOWLEDGE	Some common materials which float and sink	Effect of shape on floating and sinking, + mass	Some fish have air sacs, submarines have air tanks to inflate – to help them float
PROCESS SKILLS	Measuring, designing experiments. Predict	Recognise and predict the influence of difference variable. Formulate fair tests. Measure accurately	Recognise dependent and independent variables, and predict the relative effects of some. Look for patterns. Hypothesise. Relate their conclusion to a scientific model
ATTITUDE	Advertisements (washing powders) may only be true over limited conditions	Advertisements may mislead	

Figure 5.3   *John O'Gaunt School science department*

KNOWLEDGE:	Name the four main groups of food.
	Cut pictures of fruits and vegetables from a magazine. Label them and name your favourite.
COMPREHENSION:	Compare two green vegetables according to their shape, size, taste and how they grow.
	Cut out pictures from magazines or draw them to make a breakfast, lunch and dinner.
	Find out how many calories these foods contain.
APPLICATION:	Make a collage of foods you like to eat.
	Sow a large vegetable seed, watch it grow and draw the stage of its growth.
ANALYSIS:	List all the things that a cow gives us.
	Make up a crossword puzzle of tasty fruits. Give good clues.
SYNTHESIS:	Pretend you are a bean seed. Write a story about how you feel as you grow.
	Make up your own recipe for a really nutritious cake.
EVALUATE:	Work out how nutritional your dinner was last night.
	An apple a day keeps the doctor away. What does this saying mean?
	Don't eat between meals. Is this a good idea or not?

This worksheet is designed at Bloom's six levels of activity thus allowing any child to find a task at their right level and enable a teacher to recognise the thinking level at which the pupil is working.

Figure 5.4   *An example of Bloom's taxonomy based on topic on food for able infants*

—— CLIMBING LADDERS ——

Solving a problem like the greenhouse effect can seem so difficult that it is easier not to bother at all. But, by breaking the problem down into simple stages, it becomes possible to come up with solutions.

The example shown in the illustration below is one way of tackling the greenhouse effect. Make sure you complete each stage before going on to the next one. You may need to consult textbooks, newspapers and magazines to help you.

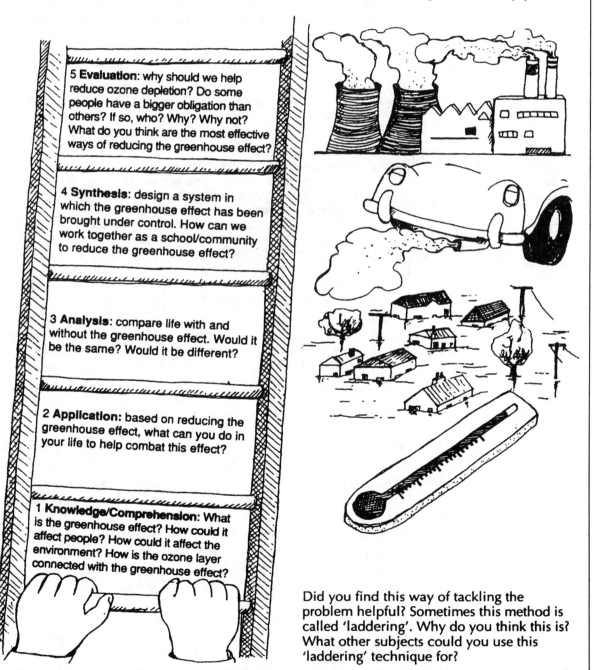

5 Evaluation: why should we help reduce ozone depletion? Do some people have a bigger obligation than others? If so, who? Why? Why not? What do you think are the most effective ways of reducing the greenhouse effect?

4 Synthesis: design a system in which the greenhouse effect has been brought under control. How can we work together as a school/community to reduce the greenhouse effect?

3 Analysis: compare life with and without the greenhouse effect. Would it be the same? Would it be different?

2 Application: based on reducing the greenhouse effect, what can you do in your life to help combat this effect?

1 Knowledge/Comprehension: What is the greenhouse effect? How could it affect people? How could it affect the environment? How is the ozone layer connected with the greenhouse effect?

Did you find this way of tackling the problem helpful? Sometimes this method is called 'laddering'. Why do you think this is? What other subjects could you use this 'laddering' technique for?

Figure 5.5   *A more advanced example of Bloom's Taxonomy (from George, 1994)*

Compacting

This is a method which allows a teacher to implement accelerative practices in the classroom. Whilst it is only a variation of individual progression, it permits students to cover a set amount of work more quickly and to use the extra time to pursue an additional activity, which should not be just more of the same. This is especially useful for teachers who are not comfortable with students being in the regular classroom and pursuing totally different work all of the time.

There are of course many variations which allow for individual progression of learning, and for flexible progression within the school's organizational structure. Research indicates that accelerated learners will usually benefit from acceleration up the school, when it is accompanied by good counselling and family involvement.

Provision and strategies for teaching

There is no single method of providing for more able children. It is advisable to consider the following factors in choosing any one method of provision:

1. Is the method flexible and open-ended enough for the child to develop at his or her own pace?
2. Does the method chosen properly emphasize the acquisition of higher order thinking skills, concepts and attitudes?
3. Does the method provide a learning environment which is as emotionally protected as it is intellectually stimulating?
4. Does the method chosen provide a process which is more valuable to the child, rather than a product which is prestigious to the school?
5. Is the method chosen likely to alienate a child from his or her peer group, and will it be detrimental to the child's subsequent learning, introducing factors which will inevitably be repeated later, which could consequently lead to boredom?

These are just some of the questions teachers should consider before adopting any one model. A model can provide a useful theoretical framework within which enriched activities can be planned. See Davis and Rimm (1989), George (1992) and George (1993) in Heller, Monks and Passow.

All teachers employ techniques and delivery systems in the classroom to provide appropriate curricula for more able children. Most instructional strategies have value in working with the more able, but those that allow for more open-ended, interactive and generatitive learning behaviours are probably most beneficial.

A variety of models have been proposed, ranging from Renzulli's Enrichment Triad Model to Guilford's Structure of the Intellect which provided a variety of thinking process, to Bloom's taxonomy which suggests that teaching involves six levels, progressing to higher level thinking. From this literature the reader can see that no one model by itself provides a comprehensive approach, and since many of the models reviewed were not developed specifically for able children, this is to be expected.

Bruce Shore (1991) of McGill University undertook a major piece of research to establish what were the most strongly supported practices for our more able children, and found there were actually very few recommended practices that are unequivocally supported. From the literature there were three that stood out: acceleration; career thinking and planning as part of the curriculum; and the need for mathematics and science to be promoted at all levels, especially for girls.

A.	HIGHER LEVEL THINKING SKILLS		
	1. Observing	7.	Collecting and organizing data
	2. Comparing	8.	Looking for assumptions
	3. Classifying	9.	Summarizing
	4. Imagining	10.	Coding
	5. Hypothesizing	11.	Interpreting
	6. Criticising	12.	Problem solving
B.	BLOOM'S TAXONOMY	(see examples of good practice, Figures 5.4 and 5.5)	
	1. Knowledge	4.	Analysis
	2. Comprehension	5.	Synthesis
	3. Application	6.	Evaluation
C.	CREATIVE THINKING		
	1. Fluency	3.	Originality
	2. Flexibility	4.	Elaboration
D.	REASONING ABILITY		
	1. Logical thinking		
	2. Problem solving		
E.	STRUCTURE OF THE INTELLECT – Operations		
	1. Cognition	4.	Convergent thinking
	2. Memory	5.	Evaluation
	3. Divergent thinking		
F.	FUTURE STUDIES		
G.	INDEPENDENT PROJECTS		
H.	FIELD TRIPS		
I.	GUEST SPEAKERS		

Table 5.1 *Enrichment programme suggestions*

Career Education – Early

The career education of these able children often begins at a younger age than that of other children, and they often aspire to careers whose name others cannot even pronounce. Their careers often involve long training which can be a constraint, especially for able girls. Shore (1991) recommends that in any programme planning for able children, a responsible advocate must include consideration of careers, beginning early; enrichment activities, to give one example, could be geared towards that end.

Mathematics and Science

In the real world these subjects are very important and present a major concern for the most able. In most careers, ignorance of science and mathematics could be a problem, and often children are both fascinated and concerned about such things as world hunger, a cure for AIDS, poverty, world pollution problems, political ethics and many others. However, there is still a concern that the National Curriculum puts too much emphasis on those subjects which are geared towards careers, to the detriment of the right brained activities which are for life and living.

The World Bank in 1993 issued the following list of industries that any country needs to develop if they are to be economically successful:

microelectronics

biotechnology

telecommunications

civilian aviation

new materials industries

robots and machine tools

computers and software.

These subjects are given a high proportion of time in the National Curriculum in maths, science and technology. There was some support from the Shore research for the following.

Future studies

Everyone is concerned about the future, and able children often enjoy its uncertainty. The future is an abstract concept and able children are often competent in dealing with such abstract thinking. Giving children the opportunity to consider solutions to future problems such as avoiding potential disasters can lend a focus for studies in ethics, civics, morals, history, mathematics as well as science. There are many positive issues that are important to discuss, and children have amazing ideas about the future of schools and what they will be like, how we will be travelling around the world, what we will be eating, weather forecasting, and even teaching!

The second recommended practice from the Shore research report is that of giving the children the opportunity to go into depth with an independent study. These children get frustrated if they have to switch subjects in a school, when they want to go into great depth. We need to give these children greater flexibility and time for these desirable activities.

The third supported practice is not academic but related to the home circumstances of these children. The practice is to be sensitive to the adjustment problems of the siblings of able children and a good working partnership with parents who are the most important teacher a child ever has. The Plowden Report states that what is important in developing the potential of all children is parental support followed by the material circumstances of the home, and only thirdly the schools.

Over the past year the author has given numerous in-service courses for teachers around Britain, following which teachers have made comments on the various ways of providing for these children in our schools. This is an impressive list, showing a great deal of concern and understanding of the problems of providing for these very able children.

● Pre-school entry. A baseline profile needed, and home visits.

● Code of practice and whole-school policy needed for able children; this could be helpful for local and national political lobbying.

● The need for good school ethos.

● Working in partnership with parents. Beware of 'over-pushy' ambitious parents.

● Counselling needed, and teachers to be available to parents perhaps once a week after school.

- Communication in school between staff, departments, years, key stages and schools. Note anecdotal evidence and the lack of frankness in the school system.
- Fostering a culture of hard work and encouragement to learn – looking forward to lessons.
- Building confidence, self-esteem – 'you are talented'.
- Profile of the whole child. Records of achievement which measure progress over a long period of time are a more sensitive way of profiling a child.
- Need for individual tutor time for guidance and counselling.
- Collate information from primary schools and all subject tutors, and then liaise with parents.
- Identify and support personal qualities such as leadership and those who care for one another.
- Have a rewards and encouragement system – not extra work as seen as punishment, but an exciting challenge.
- Do less and learn more – less repetitive practice.
- Give differentiated homework – a good option.
- Be receptive to unusual, nonconformist ideas and behaviour. Give validity to things other than writing.
- Testing, e.g. SATS, is not necessarily a good pointer.
- Need for a school coordinator.
- Review assessment system so that no child underachieves for more than a fortnight. Also grouping arrangements, e.g. concept mapping in pairs.
- Persuade colleagues and parents to acknowledge non-academic talent and provide an open-ended, broad spectrum of challenging activities.
- Ensure the affective as well as the effective curriculum is provided for.

Of course all these methods have their place but are often extra 'bolt-on' activities, whereas differentiation of lessons is the only real way to help all children reach their potential.

Acceleration

Any teaching strategy that results in advanced placement beyond a child's chronological age is called 'acceleration', and this is the most popular way to cope with more able children. The 1988 Education Reform Act assumes that most children will reach Attainment Target 6 or 7, but also that some will reach 9 or 10. Thus the Act recognizes able children who may reach this level. However, there is little cognisance of the wide abilities found in any one class of children, nor of the different needs; the curriculum content is the same for all. Our most able children have the ability to go beyond level 10.

Acceleration has been studied extensively and research on the whole has supported its use with these more able children. However, it is still a sensitive issue because too many people think it means class skipping, or 15-year-olds leaping ahead to go to college early. Of course it can mean these things, and it is interesting that many studies, even those intended to discover the dire consequences, keep confirming the success of carefully planned programmes designed to reduce the amount of time that bright children spend in school learning the same things that other children learn more slowly. Acceleration offers students the opportunity to select a programme of work that is both challenging and interesting. It is also helpful to the school because a special programme does not have to be developed and implemented for such children. These children should certainly have the opportunity to work at their own rapid pace, to progress through and out of primary school on into the secondary phase and beyond. Acceleration which speeds up learning time to match students' potential and capabilities is to be welcomed.

With early admission to the infant school, careful screening should be encouraged; yet there are still schools which do not start with a baseline of information about such children. These children will be intellectually precocious, reasonable at motor coordination, have good health, social maturity and possess adequate reading skills (see the Infant Checklist in Chapter 2). Early admission to the junior and secondary phases of education will benefit children who are ready for a more specialized course, although it may mean abandoning friends. There are, however, critics of this approach who warn of its potential problems. Some suggest that acceleration results in teaching the same material, only faster, whilst others suggest it can lead to emotional and social maladjustment. Teachers and parents are referred to the following checklist which should be carefully considered before accelerating a child, a step which may be irreversible. Perhaps most important of all, one should be aware of the differing rates of a child's development, especially emotional and social development vis-à-vis academic growth.

ACCELERATION CHECKLIST

Acceleration means
- early entry
- year-hopping
- telescoping
- compacting
- subject acceleration
- in-class acceleration
- vertical grouping

Benefits of acceleration
- improved confidence, motivation and scholarship
- helps prevent the development or habit of mental laziness
- helps to avoid underachievement and boredom
- reduces egotism and arrogance
- gives positive attitudes to learning
- allows for early completion of education

Considerations before accelerating
- gaining parental agreement and support
- is the child ready for it socially, emotionally, physically?
- readiness of child to be separated from friends
- is attainment high for age?
- seek a second opinion, e.g. educational psychologist
- anxiety and stress level, perseverance
- impact on other children in family

Eddy Braggett (1993) in Australia draws an important distinction between accelerated learners – that is children who learn faster than their age peers and are ready for more demanding work; and acceleration – which is the school's organizational response in terms of early entry, class-skipping, subject acceleration, etc. That is, a very able child will usually be an accelerated learner, though not always in school tasks, even if the school does nothing to acknowledge or accommodate this.

Early entry to school is the least obvious form of acceleration and will often be parent-initiated, but is probably not risk-free, given the problems associated with early identification. Bruce Shore (1991) suggests that it may be a more appropriate form of acceleration for girls than boys because of differences in rates of maturation and because of girls' alleged greater reluctance to be accelerated when older. Case study examples from Merica Gross's (1993) longitudinal study of highly gifted children provide living proof of the benefits of acceleration. Gross makes several important points that apply to acceleration generally, not just to those extremely gifted children who are the source of her reported findings. She confirms that acceleration does not make children conceited; gifted children can suffer anger and frustration at school, social adjustment may be impaired by not accelerating gifted children, and parents' views should be sought. Her study demonstrates that skipping the reception class year may avoid the initial frustration and dismay such children experience if expected to progress at the much slower pace of most others of their age. There is evidence of the brain drain starting early, indeed so early as one month into the infant school when the child just plays when what he or she really wants is to progress at speed.

At this point one should realize that the concept of an *accelerated learner* refers to the person, to his or her learning, and to learning outcomes. In other words, an accelerated learner is one who is moving through a programme, a module of work, a book or a study guide more quickly than others, and is now capable of more advanced thinking, understanding and content difficulty.

Acceleration, on the other hand, is usually concerned with the school's organization and with a decision about the way the school will cope with the child. The head teacher and teaching staff, hopefully in collaboration with the parents and the child, decide what type of acceleration is best for the accelerated learner in the circumstances at the time. The child who is an accelerated learner needs an appropriate acceleration programme.

There are obviously great benefits for these children from a programme acceleration:

- they can avoid or minimize the difficulties of underachievement and the ensuing boredom
- they are able to forge ahead at their own pace
- they are less likely to develop negative attitudes towards learning, the converse of which may result in satisfaction with schooling and positive attitudes towards learning
- they may study more difficult content that is appropriate to their advanced understanding
- it may also reduce the arrogance that some of these children have; they think they know it all and are not sufficiently challenged, whereas others learn to mark time and become mentally lazy.

Before we leave this topic there are two areas from the checklist that need further explanation. First, telescoping. This refers to an organizational change that the school might implement, by which a set amount of work is covered in a shorter period of time by a group of children. This is recommended as able students do not require the same intensity of consolidation and repetition, so the curriculum can be covered in a shorter period of time. It is important, however, that continuity and progress are ensured.

Second, vertical grouping. Individualized progression is very effective when it is combined with a whole-school approach of vertical grouping. This allows children of different ages to be taught together, but with all children progressing at their own pace within the group. This individualization of learning is of great benefit, but difficult to implement in a busy teacher's life. Benefits are that a child achieves higher, does more collateral reading, uses the school resources better and often has less discipline problems.

Mentoring

With the increasing pressure on teachers to differentiate the curriculum, and at the same time cope with ever-increasing class sizes, it is difficult for gifted and talented children to be given appropriate opportunity, stimulation and experiences to develop their potential and satisfy their learning needs. Mentoring of such children offers opportunities for them to interact on an individual basis with selected people for an extended time period on a topic of special interest to the child. This can be undertaken by a teacher within school time who has a similar interest and expertise, or by someone from the community appointed for such a task. In most cases, as in Canada and Australia, however, mentors are appointed to satisfy learning needs which may not easily be met in the context of the regular classroom. It is neither a remedial nor a tutorial programme, but is for those children who cannot find enough support and information at school or at home, in an area of learning which they both enjoy and want to explore further. This sharing exchange capitalizes on students' strengths and on the ability of experts.

The experience elsewhere is that each mentor involved in a programme gives their time and expertise voluntarily. The mentor meets with one or possibly a group of students outside of school hours, at regular intervals, and at a place agreed by both parties. The mentor is there to inspire and guide the student and facilitate involvement in the field of expertise. Challenging the student through open-ended discussion, observation and practice in a supportive interaction, is the essence of the mentor's role.

Like independent studies, this approach allows students to be active producers of knowledge under the guidance of an expert. Of course, teacher time is involved in finding mentors and the school needs to write to potential people in the community such as college and university lecturers, A-level teachers, service groups and community organizations such as research institutes and Rotary Clubs, cultural institutions such as museums and galleries, the media, businesses, libraries, the professions, and senior citizens. Once potential mentors have been identified it is then crucial to interview them, obtain references and, regretfully, even to check that they have no police record before appointing them. Making the best fit, both psychologically and academically, between students and mentors, can be a challenge. The scheduling of children's release time to work with an outside expert can also be a limitation, and this is why, elsewhere, most schools seem to organize the mentoring system in after-school hours. In George (1992) there is a sample letter for schools to send to parents and organizations, describing what is required by the mentoring system.

The selection of students, of course, is crucial, and the identification of these children has been described earlier. One is looking for those who have demonstrated high levels of ability, potential, and commitment in areas which they wish to pursue in depth. Children could be nominated by their parents, teachers, and themselves. They should be able to provide evidence of their ability and potential, and be motivated to pursue the area in depth with adult guidance. When nominating students for the programme, schools should consider the following points:

● they could provide evidence of work undertaken on their own behalf that demonstrated potential and ability in their area of interest or talent

● they agree to be interviewed by the programme organizer to ensure that they understood the levels of personal commitment required and the obligations of a mentor/student relationship

● successful mentor/student relationships involve students with high levels of self-motivation, and a demonstrated commitment to a particular field of study.

This work ideally needs to be undertaken by one person, who may be the coordinator for gifted and talented education in the school; sometimes this has proved to be the special needs coordinator. The major responsibilities for this person are to:

● get nominations from pupils, parents and teachers for those children who are most suitable to benefit from a mentoring system

● identify and contact mentors in the key learning areas

● build up and organize the mentor/student database

● be the coordinator of all correspondence and liaison with the school and parents

● select and interview mentors and students

● develop evaluation documents to report on the programme and individual mentor/student links

● investigate ways of assisting the mentor's link with students and their parents

● seek appropriate sponsorship for the programme. This is necessary because, although the mentoring system in my experience has not paid its mentors, there is still the expense of investigatory materials and, possibly, travel.

Some teachers will take some convincing that children will benefit from such procedures. Once they are used to compacting the curriculum, and acknowledge that these children do not need to cover all aspects of the curriculum, they can realize that it is not always possible to extend the children we have been discussing to their ultimate, but there are numerous people in the community who will be delighted to help in various ways. For example, a student could be matched up with a person who has been made redundant who has a similar enthusiasm and ability for a certain topic or subject. In the author's experience these resources are available, and indeed could be helpful to such people themselves as it would give them an interest. Where the curriculum compacting has been achieved, this mentorship model can provide a very worthwhile learning experience for our more able children. A typical scenario would be where an adult member of the community and a single student or groups of students regularly meet over a period of months, with the student possibly visiting the mentor at the job site to learn at first-hand and in detail the activities, responsibilities, problems and life-style associated with a particular business, profession or art. The school cannot expect to do everything itself in differentiating the curriculum properly, and teachers have many demands on their time, so the talent pool of the community should be seen as a vital potential resource, and is commended.

Conclusion

Teachers on in-service courses were asked what was most important in providing for our most able children. Their replies, shown in Table 5.2, are ranked and it is noticeable that teachers come top of the table, which is understandable given that they are 80 per cent of the average school budget; this is followed by differentiation.

Feature	Total rank value
1. The teacher	274
2. The curriculum: purposefully distinctive	240
3. Student selection procedures	220
4. A statement of philosophy and objectives	208
5. Staff orientation	200
6. A plan of evaluation	139
7. Administrative responsibility	125
8. Guidance services	95
9. Ability grouping and/or acceleration	92
10. Special equipment and facilities	73
11. Use of community resources	50
12. Early admission	41
13. Community interpretation	40
14. Supplementary expenditures	35
15. A programme of research	25

Table 5.2 *Key features in programmes for the most able*

Teaching strategies for 'gifted' and very able pupils

- Using the pupils themselves
- Open competition
- Using the pupil as the teacher
- Using yourself as a resource
- Designing a new curriculum
- Making better use of the school's facilities

- Using the teacher's special interests
- Special school or class responsibilities
- Special homework *(the best way of establishing individual learning)*
- Language classes
- Master classes
- Specialized training courses
- Extra-curricular provision
- Extra-mural support
  - local colleges and university faculties
  - specialist organizations
  - talented parents
- Pupils becoming their own teachers
  - pupils devising the next stages in their learning programmes; the next stage in their projects, their own work sheets
  - pupils predict/devise the next stages for class projects
- Social programmes
  - cooperative work programmes
  - sensitivity games
  - building confidence in front of an audience
  - self-critical tasks
- Dialogue and planned cooperation between teachers and parents
- Observational pairings.

CHAPTER 6

Differentiation

Treat people as if they were what they ought to be and you help them to become what they are capable of being.

(Goethe)

A curriculum which is differentiated for every pupil will build on past achievements; present challenges to allow for more achievements; provide opportunity for success; and remove barriers to participation.

This means teachers devising tasks appropriate to the range of abilities, aptitudes and interests of their children; regularly reviewing pupils' progress through observation, discussion and testing, which leads to variation in the tasks pupils have to undertake; and teachers offering support for individual work, both in person and through the ready availability of appropriate resources.

This word 'differentiation' has become a live issue because schools experience difficulty in coping effectively with the wide range of pupils that come through their doors. The spread of comprehensive schools and the increasing access to mainstream schools of pupils who have quite acute learning or behavioural difficulties, has highlighted an issue that has always been there. The mixed ability groups, taken for granted and, on the whole, well executed in primary schools, are seen by some as a threat to standards in the secondary school. There has been a long-running debate about standards, which shows no sign of diminishing. For some, the solution lies in the return to grammar schools, which for those who thrived in them were often a great success, but there was also a great deal of underachievement in the old tripartite system, just as there undoubtedly is in many a comprehensive school today. To link differentiation to pupils at the extremes of the normal distribution curve of ability is to miss the point. No mass of 60 per cent of our pupils in the middle range are doing well in our schools. Some are, but many are not. Differentiation is not primarily about helping slow learners or disaffected pupils. Differentiation is not just about stretching the clever child. Differentiation is about *all* children, because all children are different, and one of the fascinating aspects of being a teacher is this very fact of human variation and all its attributes. Differentiation then is the process by which curriculum objectives, teaching methods, assessment methods, resources and learning activities are planned to cater for the needs of individual pupils. Differentiation is making the whole curriculum accessible to all individuals in ways which meet their learning needs. This is as good a definition as any. With this definition in mind, it then becomes the lynchpin of the entitlement curriculum: it is meaningless if access is not available. The other important point about this definition is the emphasis on the individual, which could prove to be much more helpful than using categories like slow learner, average, bright or gifted (although it would be foolish to suggest that these categories are meaningless). They are all marked by individuality: our children think differently, behave differently, learn differently, come from different backgrounds and bring different skills, attitudes and abilities with them. This is both the joy and the great challenge for the busy teacher. For this reason, I regard differentiation as an issue affecting all pupils of every age in every school in every kind of grouping, and this is what makes the teaching profession such a skilled pursuit.

Definitions

The process whereby teachers match the need for progress through the curriculum, and by the selection of appropriate teaching methods for an individual child within a group situation (Visser)

Differentiation is a planned process of intervention in the classroom to maximize potential, based on individual needs (George)

Policies of special education needs and the effectiveness of the curricula and other provision which stems from them, including assessment of individual needs, differentiated teaching, meeting the requirements or statements for those pupils concerned (OFSTED, 1993)

The aims of using differentiation in your teaching should be:

● to raise the achievement of all pupils

● to ensure success for all pupils, so that they reach their own personal best performance.

67

Some differences between pupils are in:

- ability
- aptitude
- personality and attitude
- gender
- race and culture
- learning style and speed of learning

- prior learning
- reading skills
- motivation
- home background
- physical attributes
- capability.

MANAGING DIFFERENTIATION: WORKSHEET

In your teaching practice, have you considered any or all of the following strategies for improving access to the curriculum for able children, indeed *all* children? (Mark along the line where you think you are:

◀ ----- A little . . . A lot ------------ ▶)

This term (choose any three-week period) I have used the following approaches:

1. Didactic exposition _____
2. Whole-class teaching _____
3. Individual work_____
4. Small-group work _____
5. Partner work _____
6. Visual material _____
7. Audio tapes/discs_____
8. Role play/simulation _____
9. Drama _____
10. Questions at differing levels_____
11. Silent reading _____
12. Group discussions_____
13. Survey/questionnaire techniques _____
14. Practical experiments _____
15. Work pitched at several levels of response _____
16. Varied pupil groupings_____
17. Guest teachers/other adults _____
18. Differentiated homework_____
19. Negotiated approaches with pupil directing _____
20. Contexts outside school, e.g. community, theatre visits, etc.

_____

AND add your own

Points for discussion
Do you have a dominant profile? What do your results show you about your teaching style? Discuss these with a friend or peer group. Which strategies are most important for meeting individual needs? Ask a colleague to observe your teaching as a follow-up.

A checklist can provide a series of clues as to what is or is not happening, and a checklist such as that which follows, used in conjunction with other forms of evaluation, can help improve a school's effectiveness.

Dr Mary Saunders of the University of Lancaster suggests performance indicators are useful in evaluating work being achieved, and provide evidence of something being done. She suggests three types of performance indicators:

Enabling indicators – evidence of things put in place to enable something to happen.

Process indicators – evidence of what is actually happening.

Outcome indicators – evidence that what is happening is producing good results.

The following list has been adapted and hopefully improved, but came originally from a group of teachers considering differentiation in their schools, and published by Essex TVEI.

GOOD PRACTICE CHECKLIST

Enabling indicators which imply thorough planning and preparation:

- Clear learning objectives.

- A variety of reading levels within text resources, starting in the early crucial years.

- A variety of differentiated resources available.

- A variety of tasks set – content beyond the National Curriculum starting at the right level of competence.

- Teacher language accessible to all pupils and certainly upgrading for the most able, especially girls.

- Clear communication between parents, pupils and teachers.

- Open-ended questions and methods of questioning accessible to all pupils – 'Judicious questioning is nearly the half of knowledge'.

- Accepting and valuing the attitudes of pupils.

- Different forms of grouping of children, e.g. in pairs for concept mapping.

- Differentiated materials readily available.

- The use of non-textual resources such as audio-visual aids.

- Non-teaching assistants and mentors from the community available to give support.

- Creative learning environment – school ethos – policy.

- Good and varied methods of assessment in order to spot underachievement.

- Teachers aware of pupils' prior learning and experiences from class to class, key stage to key stage, school to school.

- Clear presentation of tasks set.

- Flexible deadlines set for completion of work.

- Challenging and different homework.

- Ongoing education for all staff.

Process indicators – the journey the children make through their learning:

- Multi-sensory approach.
- Children given the chance to work independently on a wide variety of tasks.
- Children making their own decisions.
- Children working in a variety of ways.
- Classroom organized by grouping of children appropriate for that topic.
- Children working on a variety of tasks at different levels, especially higher level cognitive processes.
- The involvement of all pupils – motivation.
- Variety of resources in use.
- Pupils on task and the teacher aware of any difficulties.
- Good child/teacher interaction and in partnership with parents.
- Children involved in negotiating their work, and good child-to-child interaction.
- Children involved in negotiating their work and presenting outcomes in a variety of ways, not just writing it down. Therefore a variety of assessment techniques in use and children working on time.
- Cooperative working and learning taking place.
- Appropriate worksheets and guides in use – see Bloom's *Taxonomy*.
- Open-ended questions.

Outcome indicators – able children should produce work of a quality in accordance with their abilities:

- Development of thinking skills and problem-solving ability.
- A variety of outcomes.
- Celebrating success and good scholarship.
- Improved achievement with different outcomes from different children.
- Improved behaviour and motivation and less discipline problems.
- More collateral reading taking place, using all school resources better.
- Improved school results.
- Better understanding by pupils of subject matter.
- Good attitudes towards work, school and peer group.
- A variety of completed tasks.
- Children able to plan for the next stage of learning and eager for the next lesson.
- Less teacher stress and reduced truancy rates.
- Better attentive development.
- Greater awareness of pupils' needs and abilities on behalf of the teachers.
- Pupil awareness of purpose and objectives of the work they are doing.
- Improved whole-school ethos.

From my experience with both pupils and teachers, there are two models which can be recommended to start differentiating in the classroom: Bloom's

Taxonomy and the 'Must, Should and Could' grid, which were illustrated earlier in the book. They are not too time-consuming and back-up resources are available.

Of course differentiation is all about how children learn and how we teach. The research shown in Figure 6.1 is very challenging for any teacher in considering how to teach our different children.

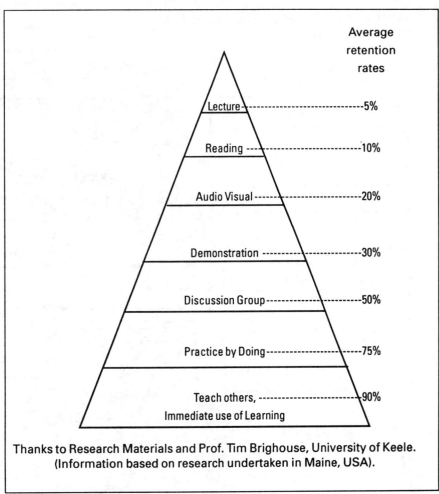

Figure 6.1   *The learning pyramid*

Turning teacher

The author has recently written a book of enrichment activities for able children (George, 1994) and the following is an example from this, whereby the teacher puts the onus on the child to come up with an interesting topic for learning (see Figure 6.2).

The aim is to allow students to explore the challenge of devising and managing their own learning processes, during which they should come to understand some of the difficulties involved in producing themed, coherent classwork. Children may work on their own, but small groups of students may be able to devise a wider range of topics. Some of the possible areas of study, determined from the starter worksheet in Figure 6.2, could include the following:

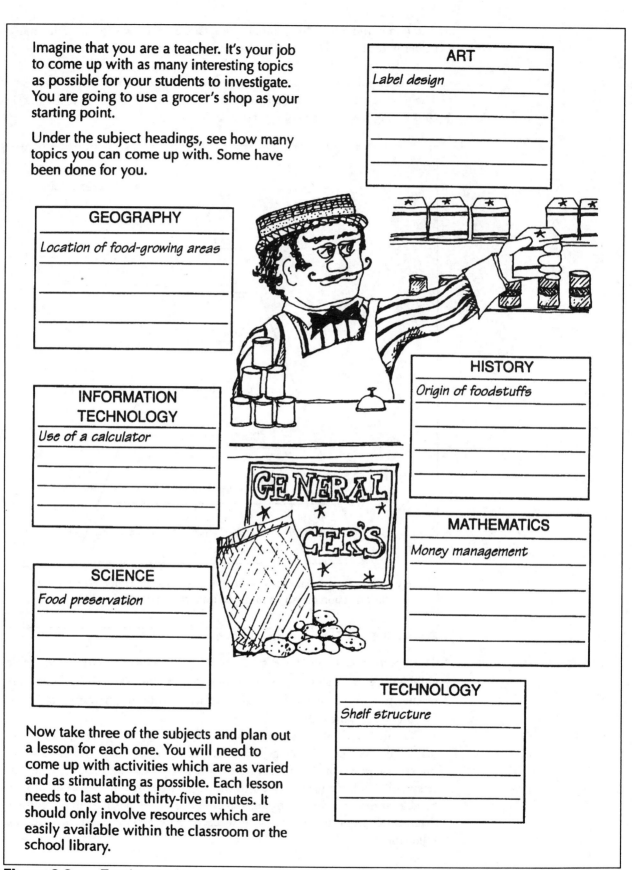

Imagine that you are a teacher. It's your job to come up with as many interesting topics as possible for your students to investigate. You are going to use a grocer's shop as your starting point.

Under the subject headings, see how many topics you can come up with. Some have been done for you.

ART

Label design

GEOGRAPHY

Location of food-growing areas

INFORMATION TECHNOLOGY

Use of a calculator

HISTORY

Origin of foodstuffs

SCIENCE

Food preservation

MATHEMATICS

Money management

TECHNOLOGY

Shelf structure

Now take three of the subjects and plan out a lesson for each one. You will need to come up with activities which are as varied and as stimulating as possible. Each lesson needs to last about thirty-five minutes. It should only involve resources which are easily available within the classroom or the school library.

Figure 6.2   *Turning teacher*   *(Reprinted from George, 1994, with permission.)*

Geography: climate and crop growth, transport and cost of goods.

Information technology: checkout tills, bar codes.

Science: nutritional needs, food values, sexual and asexual reproduction in plants, cultivation, improvement of crop yield, ecology, danger of overcropping, additives in food.

Art: aesthetics of natural forms, design, packaging and advertising.

History: countries of origin of our plants, anthropology and social structure of countries of origin.

Mathematics: weight, size and shape of goods, stock control, cash flow, energy budgets.

Technology: principles of refrigeration, structure of shelving, mechanics of packaging, loads.

Another example of an enrichment activity deals with concept mapping in the humanities. Pupils were asked what they would like to study about buildings. Figures 6.3 and 6.4 show two different approaches by two girls working in pairs, and are good examples of differentiation by outcome.

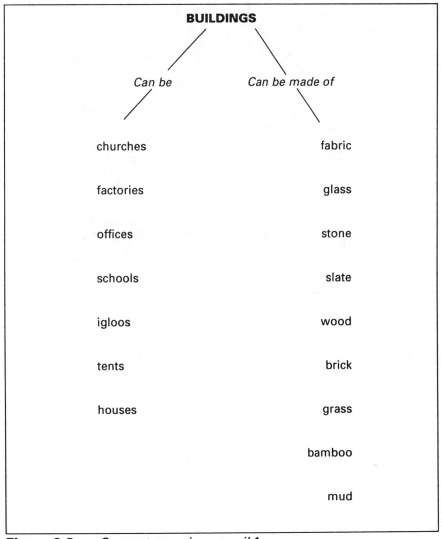

Figure 6.3   *Concept mapping – pupil 1*

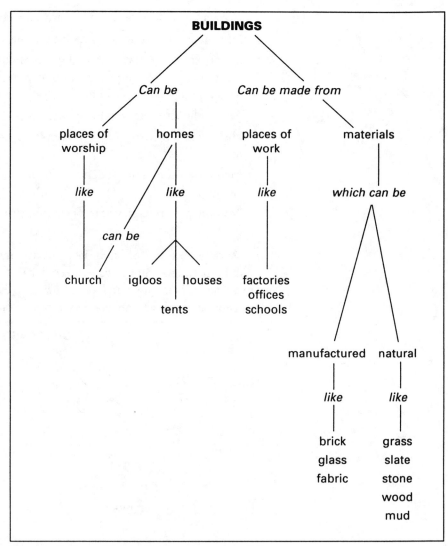

Figure 6.4   *Concept mapping – pupil 2*

CHAPTER 7

Affective Learning

After you understand about the sun and the stars and the rotation of the earth, you may still miss the radiance of the sunset.
(AW Whitehead)

Whatever school prospectus one looks at, one immediately sees that there is a broad category in all school aims and objectives which can be called 'the affective curriculum'. This includes students' self-concepts, self-esteem, moral thinking, attitudes, values, social and personal adjustment, self-motivated learning, and such interrelated humanistic matters as self-actualization and a democratic concern for the welfare of others.

Some teachers will immediately throw their hands up in horror and say, 'Do I have to teach this, and if so how, and in what time?' There is no doubt about it that the above areas are essential in order to help all children reach their potential as well-rounded people, and we could well argue that this is the responsibility of parents. However, there is evidence of parents abdicating their responsibility for such matters, so the author considers it an essential part of an holistic school-based education for all our children. Indeed, most schools would include the following in their aims and objectives;

● We care for children and their needs, talents, and wide interests throughout their school career.

● Every child has individual gifts and abilities, and our school recognizes this and helps children to realize their potential in a happy, caring working atmosphere. Therefore the school agreed the following aims:
  – To provide a secure, stimulating, disciplined environment in which pupils can develop an enquiring attitude and achieve high standards of work.
  – To foster a genuine partnership between home and school.
  – To encourage all members of the school community to show a proper consideration for each other, based on mutual and self respect.
  – To develop pupils as individuals by offering a broad and balanced curriculum.
  – To encourage full participation and strive for excellence in academic, sporting and artistic endeavours.
  – To encourage children to develop interests through extracurricular activities within both school and community.
  – To help pupils to begin to prepare themselves for the opportunities, experiences, responsibilities and duties of adult life. (Hexham Middle School)

These are very laudable aims, and the emphasis is on the whole child, but there is nothing about the school being in partnership with the parents. After all, children are only in school 17 per cent of their waking life, and therefore the most important teacher the child ever has is the parents. HMI Pecker in the Plowden Report (1953) emphasized that the three priorities for helping all children to reach their potential are as follows:

● Good parenting.

● Home material circumstances – and he went on to explain that this did not mean a stereo and television in every room in the house etc, but quality of books, selective television viewing, educational visits, perhaps above all language. (The average American parents talk to their children 20 minutes a week; as far as one knows similar research has not been undertaken in Britain.) Next to security, love and food, the most important thing for a child is language.

● Third, and only third, are good schools.

This research was repeated in 1993 by NFER who came to the same conclusion.

An excellent book was published in 1993, entitled *Talented Teenagers*, by Csikszentmihalyi *et al.* These American professors undertook research amongst an equal number of boys and girls in the age range 13 to 14, looked at those who achieved highly in art, athletics, mathematics, music and science, and came to the following conclusions:

● Teenagers must develop skills that can be recognized.

● Appropriate or supportive personality traits recognized in the successful teenagers were energy, endurance, openness and responsiveness.

● Productive habits:
  – limited socializing
  – concentration on school as their main focus in life
  – time to be alone
  – no after-school jobs
  – as much interaction with parents as possible
  – limited TV viewing.

● Conservative sexual attitudes.

● As much family support as possible, in families that are cohesive and flexible and where parents model discipline, intellectuality and productivity.

● Teachers who were good role models, who had a romance with their discipline, had a professional identity, and were involved in their field.

● Teenagers required rewards and recognition.

● Talent and talent development are complex processes which necessitate both differentiation and integration of the curriculum.

This sounds very idealistic, but one has to be optimistic if we are to fully help these children in our care.

Much has been written about differentiation: the differences between pupils, the differences in how children learn and in how we teach. From the above, one can now add to those differences topics such as the social and cultural gap between children and their families; limited receptiveness, possibly resulting from a child being allowed to stay up and watch the midnight movie and then missing breakfast; negative attitudes and low expectations, insufficient emphasis on education from parents, and contradictory messages from parents and some teachers as well as members of the peer group.

All this means that schools, in conjunction with parents, need to develop a philosophy which is based on the belief of self-actualization, which respects the growth and uniqueness of each child in the community as well as the reality of mutual interdependence. Most schools in this country now have a policy of teaching perhaps two lessons a week on what is commonly called 'personal health and social education'. The philosophy needs to permeate the whole, as it only becomes reality through its implementation. It is valid if it permeates every aspect of the particular educational establishment, without exception. It is a concept of the individual and of self-actualization for all, as opposed to the concept of education for outside success where the primary focus is on what one can do rather than what one is as a human being.

I am convinced that the success model of traditional Western education has resulted in developing people who are highly capable, but has failed in satisfying peoples' needs for self-actualization and learning how to become participating members in an interdependent community.

Our society has made two promises to its children. The first is to prepare a world which accepts them and provides them with opportunities to live, grow and create in safety. The other is to help them develop their whole beings to the fullest in every respect. Education is the vehicle through which we try to keep these promises, in partnership with parents.

The success and failure of our education system is a source of endless debate. The 'back to basics' movement was expected to solve all problems for ever, as was the National Curriculum with its testing system and levels. Yet still there is great dissatisfaction with our education system. The newspapers are filled with reports of low test results and the lack of skills and information among our children, which are interpreted as failures of education yet again. In addition, we hear about social problems such as drug abuse, delinquency, dropouts, vandalism, depression and suicide.

Society looks for the culprit in many places, such as permissive child rearing, second-rate teacher training, mediocre teachers, lack of resources, low teacher salaries, large class sizes – one could go on. All this results in increased pressure on children and teachers, more demands to conform, more emphasis on the three Rs and skills education. In many ways this is unfair to our educational system and to so many devoted teachers, pointing to the symptoms without taking the time and thought to determine and treat the underlying cause.

We are living in a world which is much more interdependent, and this calls for a change in our approach to education. However, because education is still based on tradition, this is not happening in any fundamental way. We are not looking at the purposes of education, which are for life and for living, but are putting more emphasis on education for jobs. We continue to educate for the next step, the next test, the next class, the next key stage and the next school. This leads to education in isolated fragments and we fail to bind the fragments together into a meaningful continuum.

We need to ask questions, such as have we examined the cause and effect of our educational processes realistically? Have we looked at the adults that our system has produced? Are they healthy, wealthy and wise? Are they using their full potential? Are they equipped to deal with modern life? I think that we have raised illiterates when it comes to mastering the science or art of living: yet education should encourage children to prepare for life.

We assume that all children learn in the same manner, that they are vessels to be filled; the essential ingredient for learning is seen as the activity of teaching rather than the child as learner and grower. It seems to me that we are going backwards in our whole approach, which says to a child, 'You are a passive recipient, not an active participant in your learning process'. We ignore the hidden curricula, which probably have a more permanent and integrative impact on a child than that provided by the school.

Space does not allow me to pursue this important issue much further, but I make some suggestions in Table 7.1 for the development of the 'self'. The table suggests aspects of personal and social development which are an essential part of the education of whole people, and needs to be considered in partnership with parents.

Bodily Self	understanding changes and their variety, reflecting on the impact of these, addressing the use and misuse of the body, including substance abuse
Sexual Self	understanding sexual development, the role of sexuality in relationships
Social Self	understanding others' perspectives, their role in relationships, making sense of others and their judgements, coping with conflicts, presenting oneself in a range of situations, working with others
Vocational Self	developing awareness of adult roles, lifestyles and preferences, valuing a range of contributions, transition to adult role
Moral/Political Self	the making of judgements, resolving moral dilemmas, taking action on issues
Self as a Learner	understanding strengths and weaknesses, reflecting on approaches to learning
Self in the Organization	becoming an active member of the school, making sense of the organization and getting the most from it

Figure 7.1   *Aspects of personal and social development; the whole child*

Enhancing self-esteem   In the classroom, teachers need to provide opportunities for children to work together and undertake trust activities where they can express their feelings. This is often provided in drama lessons and religious education. Children need to have the opportunity for positive feedback activities, risk-taking exercises, self-recording and evaluation to include pupils initiating their own learning.

A school policy needs to give attention to enhancing the self-esteem of all enable them to be good role models for all pupils, and to develop a clear and consistent policy for the management of pupil behaviour. We need to adopt a policy for mediation that ensures pupil disputes can be heard, and an active policy of parental involvement. The provision of lunchtime activities and dinner arrangements that allow for staff and pupils' contact in a family setting, is invaluable.

Earlier in this book readers were given a checklist to help identify our gifted and talented children; here is another checklist to pick out the characteristics we have discussed in this chapter.

PERSONAL AND SOCIAL DEVELOPMENT CHECKLIST

Appreciates social values
1. Senses right and wrong.
2. Requests the right of others.
3. Contributes constructively to group activities.
4. Is willing to share.
5. Is conscientious and truthful.

Establishes good relationships.
1. Has self-respect.
2. Has keen sense of humour.
3. Has permanence of mood.
4. Is friendly, helpful and cooperative.

Figure 7.2 presents a model of the whole environment in which children, parents and teachers interact. In an earlier book (George, 1994) I presented able children with a worksheet which helps them to come to terms with their whole self; this holistic worksheet is included here (see Figure 7.3) as an example of good practice for children. In addition, readers are referred to Maslow's 'hierarchy of human needs' (1954). This model asserts that it is necessary that an individual's basic needs are satisfied before higher levels can be met, and suggests that emotions reflect the level of satisfaction which an individual experiences. The aim is that we should help children go from the base of their pyramid, where basic needs are physiological, to the top of the pyramid which is self-actualization. (There follows a simple worksheet for children to tackle, based on this premise.) When basic needs are met, motivation will direct behaviour towards fulfilling the higher-level needs: the need to live up to one's fullest and unique potential, to know and understand, and the need for beauty and order in one's life. (For activities in addition to those shown on the following pages, see George, 1994.)

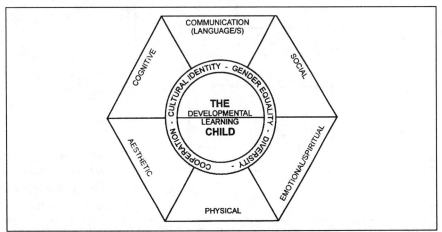

Figure 7.2   *A holistic model of the parent/child/teacher environment*

Who you are depends on lots of different things. For instance, there is a 'you' who gets colds, a 'you' who is shy and a 'you' who goes swimming every week.

In the five boxes around the illustration, fill in as many words as possible which describe the different aspects of your personality.

Are there any other aspects of yourself which you would like to include?

SPIRITUAL

EMOTIONAL

MENTAL

PHYSICAL

SOCIAL

Now that you have plenty of words which describe every aspect of your life, write a poem which explains your personality and your lifestyle, and includes your name.

Figure 7.2   *'Who are you?' worksheet. Reprinted with permission from George (1994)*

'What Children Really Want' Worksheet

The Swiss, who managed to stay out of the Second World War itself, sent their health workers out to begin tackling some of the problems caused by the war; one man, a doctor, was given the job of researching how best to care for the orphan babies.

He travelled about Europe and visited many kinds of orphan-care situations, to see what was the most successful type of care. He saw many extremes. In some places, American field hospitals had been set up and the babies were snug in stainless steel cots, in hygienic wards, getting their four-hourly feeds of special milk formula from white-uniformed nurses.

At the other end of the scale, in remote mountain villages, a truck had simply pulled up, the driver had asked, 'Can you look after these babies?' and left half a dozen crying infants to the care of the villagers. Here, surrounded by kids, dogs, goats, in the arms of the village women, the babies took their chances on goats' milk and the communal stewpot.

The Swiss doctor had a simple way of comparing the different forms of care. No need even to weigh the babies, far less measure coordination or look for smiling and eye contact. In those days of influenza and dysentery, he used the simplest of all statistics – the death rate.

And what he discovered was rather a surprise.... As epidemics raged through Europe and many people were dying, the children in the rough villages were thriving better than their scientifically-cared-for counterparts in the hospitals!

The doctor had discovered something that old wives had known for a long time (but – since they were only women – no one had really listened to them). He had discovered that babies need *love* to live.

The infants in the field hospital had everything but affection and stimulation. The babies in the villages had more hugs, bounces and things to see than they knew what to do with and, given reasonable basic care, were thriving.

Of course, the doctor didn't use the word *'love'* (words like that upset scientists) but he spelt it out clearly enough. What was important, he said, was: skin to skin contact, eye to eye contact.

When do you really feel good and comfortable with yourself? There follow two suggestions to help you discover yourself and reach your potential as a whole person.

Where Do I Go From Here?
'Life is something that happens to you while you are busy making other plans' – John Lennon.

Spend a few moments thinking about what you would like to be doing in five years time.

To plan the future we need to decide on the things in life that are important, so that we can work to improve ourselves. One way of looking at people's lives is found in the work of a psychologist ABRAHAM MASLOW. He described people's needs by saying they were like a triangle with different levels. Every human being starts at the bottom, but fewer and fewer people manage to get from each level to the next.

The bottom level is our most *basic* need – food and drink for survival. Next comes *safety* so that we can feel secure. The need to be *loved and belong* comes next and above that is the need for *respect* which comes from the feeling that we have achieved things – followed by freedom to learn, beauty and order until we reach our *true potential.*

The second suggestion has already been shown, as Figure 7.2.

Maslow's Triangle

Few reach their true potential

Self concept

Some enjoy beauty

Some are free to learn

Some are respected

We need to be loved

We search for a safe place to live

We all need food and drink

Classwork:

(1) Explain in your own words what Maslow's Triangle describes.

(2) Write down a 'Plan of Action' to enable you to reach your goal in five years time.

(3) What do you think is the most important decision you have made in your life so far? What will be your next important decision?

(4) Describe the people/events which could shape your future.

CHAPTER 8

Policies

In order to offer an effective service in meeting the needs of more able children in our schools, governors, parents, teachers and other involved professionals need to be clear about what school policies exist in general, and what policy there is in particular for these children. These children should be educated in a way which enables them to work at the highest level concomitant with their ability and interest, both for the good of others and for their own satisfaction. It is generally recognized that those of exceptional high ability, in whatever area of human endeavour, require rich challenging experiences to achieve their potential.

Schools should have clear policies on meeting the needs of pupils, including ways of identifying and monitoring their progress and making provision that is consonant with the National Curriculum, but which also enriches, extends and differentiates it. (For more details see George, 1992.)

In devising a policy for meeting the needs of our more able children, one should expect to see:

● Consistent terminology and definition. For Britain, where a National Curriculum is in place, a definition might well be as follows:

Gifted and talented children are those students whose functioning is at least at the upper end or above that normally associated with that key stage, and whose abilities are so well developed or so far in advance of their peer group, that a school has to provide additional learning experiences which develop, enhance and extend the identified abilities.

This definition should then be accompanied by a profile of the child, which will assist the teacher to consider the first stage of identification. The school then needs to consider, 'Have we any children like this? How are we meeting their needs?'

● Senior management defining and agreeing methods for screening, registering and monitoring the progress of pupils with these abilities.

● Advice on identifying gifted and talented children.

● Aims and objectives which reflect the idea that the provision for able children should be seen as an aspect of provision for all pupils. Therefore it is important to raise the awareness of all staff, and for management to provide training and guidance to enable all teachers to meet the needs of these children.

- Staff having a sense of ownership of the policy, through reaching agreement on the appropriate procedures for recognition, provision and assessment of children.

- Teachers providing opportunities for pupils to practise and develop their particular abilities, so that the children who have these abilities are provided with opportunities to get together to share and develop their talents; this can be provided in a variety of ways.

- A directory of useful local expertise which may assist these children in their work, including the appointment of mentors.

- Pupils working, for the most part, with their peers in ways that lead to social and emotional maturity and which help them to build strong relationships with others. They should have the opportunity to work in great depth at times.

- A collection of appropriate differentiated resources.

- Records which monitor the progress of the children identified.

The Role of the School Coordinator

Once a policy has been agreed, it is then essential to have a school coordinator appointed; such a person needs highly developed perception and communication skills. In my experience such a role often befalls the special needs coordinator, who has more than enough to do, and a case needs to be made for a person to be appointed to coordinate the work for the most able.

Such a coordinator would have the following role in the school:

- Initiating the formulation and revision of the school policy.

- Consulting with the senior management of the school and all the staff.

- Ensuring that the governors inform parents about the school's policies for the more able children, with clear statements in the prospectus (see DfE Circulars 4/93 and 5/93).

- Ensuring that there is good liaison with the parents of the more able children.

- Seeing that all areas of the National Curriculum and beyond are planned with a suitably differentiated curriculum for the more able child.

- Ensuring that the development of colleagues is enabled via in-service training of a national, county or in-house nature. This is particularly important for new colleagues, as few teachers have had training in the identification and needs of more able children.

- Calling for nominations of able children from staff, parents and students.

- Identifying, inviting, interviewing and matching mentors to students, and arranging an initial meeting between students, mentors and parents.

- Initiating and maintaining an agreed system of profiling, including testing.

- Establishing systems for cross-phase liaison, so that teachers talk to each other about able children.

- Regularly following up students' progress with mentors, supervising teachers and students.

- Being responsible for building up a resource bank of differentiated materials which are readily accessible to the more able.

- Ensuring that the resources of the wider community are exploited positively, e.g. libraries, learned societies, museums, volunteer adults.

● Being the liaison person with national organizations such as NACE and NAGC; attending the national conferences and being aware of support systems available.

In addition to the above, secondary schools should have within each department a nominated lead person who would develop subject-specific criteria for the identification of the more able, and ensure that all subject specialists steadily increase their awareness of the needs of the more able and how they are to be provided for.

It is also suggested that the nominated coordinator for the more able should chair a school committee for this work. A suggested agenda for early meetings would be as follows.

● How can this be planned, managed and delivered?

● How can we extend the way children are involved in their own learning?

● How can children be given even more responsibility for their own learning?

● How can we extend our cross-phase links to encompass tutoring?

● How can the library service help to supplement our resources?

● Have we a targeted plan for resource buying?

One of the great pleasures of undertaking in-service courses around the country is that following a course, most schools then implement policies and a plan of action to support teachers and their more able children in schools. This has also meant that a number of schools have sent the author materials and policies as well as action plans. The author is grateful for permission to use the following papers from several schools around Britain, which vary from rural to urban, primary to secondary, as well as in approach and level of success to date. These are examples for other schools to emulate.

Snodland Primary School, School policy on the able child

Definition

Any definition by its very nature will be subject to criticism and individual interpretation. `Gifted` is a term which can be used to refer to children at the extreme range of ability (the top 2 per cent) within one subject or across several.

As a staff, we feel that the definition of gifted should include the able top 20

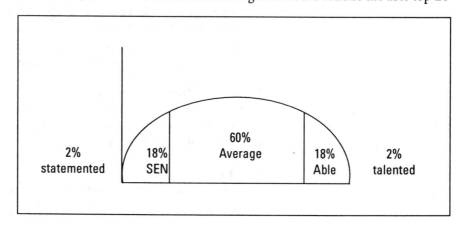

per cent in the standard distribution curve of ability: a proportionate number to the children whose needs are met in our special needs policy.

This means that on average, in a class of 30, there should be about six children who fall into this category. Within our 14 classes we are looking at identifying and providing for 80 to 90 children.

Of all the definitions we have examined, that which best covers our requirements is David George's (1992):

> Gifted and talented children are those who in some aspect of human potential and/or achievement are far more advanced beyond that which would normally be expected.

This broad, general definition covers potential achievement in intellectual ability, creativity, leadership, visual and performing arts and psycho-motor ability, and thereby provides many opportunities for children to have access to our provision of extension and enrichment.

Identification

> There are a number of possible methods of identification. All of them have weaknesses and limitations. It is sensible, therefore, to use as wide a net as possible, incorporating many strands of thought, and not to rely too heavily upon the results of any one method. (Teare, 1988)

Methods of identification

Norm Referenced Tests
These can be useful as an initial screen to supplement and counterbalance teacher observations. They may not identify those with motivational or observational problems.

Checklists – General Characteristics
Useful as a guide on what to look for. They may not be relevant in individual cases.

Creativity Tests
These may offer the chance to show quality of imagination and divergent thinking in those overlooked by conventional tests. These are difficult to assess and time-consuming to administer

Teacher Observation and Recommendations
These are essential: the trained eye of the teacher should know the child, but may miss some who do not conform to accepted standards of work or behaviour; who present motivational or behavioural problems; with belligerent or apathetic attitudes; who come from homes which do not share the school ethos.

Creative Learning Environment
The all-important ingredient, encouraging all children to explore their talents, exercise their developing capacity to learn and understand, and to reach the highest potential of which they are capable.

Provision
Provision for the able child will focus on three areas: material, organizational and pedagogic.

Material

Children will have access to further reading material, extra source material of all kinds to facilitate deeper and more detailed study of the theme in hand. Individual learning packs or assignment sheets from a variety of sources will be readily available to enrich the normal supply of classroom materials as well as the class teacher's own produced materials.

Organizational

Provision to enrich or extend the curriculum may include extra individual or group help *in situ* by a visiting teacher; withdrawal from the normal class to take part individually or as a group in curricular studies; promotion for part or whole of the week regularly/occasionally to work with a more advanced class; visits to exhibitions, museums, field centres; visits by poets, painters, etc.

Pedagogic

Pedagogic provision lies at the heart of enrichment and extension. it represents the personal element upon which all depends. The inspirational mentor, the gifted teacher, can offer more than any amount of inanimate material and organization. Staff INSET, both present and future, will help to ensure that this aspect of provision remains firmly fixed as part of this policy and our overall school philosophy.

Recommendations

In order to recommend a child for able provision, teachers will need to provide a record of their observations. Observation and recording of such children need to be as objective as possible, and it will therefore help to have a structured framework within which such observations can be formulated.

a. Evidence from school tests
   - any child who scores 115 or more on any of the NFER tests
   - any child who scores 120 or more on the intelligence test
   - any child whose reading age is one year or more above their chronological age.

b. Teacher referral checklist
   - any child who has a majority of ticks in the exceptional category.

c. Any other evidence not covered in a. or b., but which is considered by the class teacher to be indicative of above-average ability.

This evidence to be submitted on referral form to the Able Child Coordinator.

Examples of identification material:

Norm Referenced Tests	NFER English
	NFER Maths
	NFER Reading
	Hunter Grundin Reading Intelligence Test.
Checklist of General Characteristics	From 'Teaching Bright Pupils', Nottingham University School of Education.
Creativity Test	TCT – DP/TSD Z Testsheet from Urban and Jellen.
Referral Form and Teachers' Checklist.	

Whickham Comprehensive School, 1994/95 Development Plan: Very Able Children

Rationale

School aims:

A.7.　　...we should encourage realistically high expectations in pupils of all abilities...to the highest standards from the 'gifted' pupils.

B.8.　　...there should be sufficient differentiation to...challenge all pupils, not least the very able.

Policy Statement: Very Able Children

We shall, by suitable means, identify children of exceptional ability or talent on entry to the school. Such children shall be monitored throughout their time at school, and shall be provided with an educational experience which will challenge them and stimulate their development.

The identification strategy shall be broad, encompassing cognitive, creative and special talents. The strategy will also take account of maturation and so be flexible, allowing students to be added or withdrawn from the identified cohort as our knowledge of each year group develops. Linked to identification and monitoring will be a review process carried out by Heads of House and coordinated by a senior teacher.

Provision for the very able will take the form of differentiated work within subject departments, and a programme of enrichment activities provided by a support team.

Identification and monitoring

Very able children are usually identified by the class teacher, and observations are shared and discussed with parents, the headteacher and coordinator. Appropriate action is then agreed and undertaken. Referral to outside agencies may take place with parental permission; this could be the Support Service, Educational Psychologist or an independent educational consultant.

Action for the future

Set up a formal process twice a term between headteacher, coordinator and staff to review:

a. Present children in the group.

b. Identifying new children.

Work schedule and targets for individual children would also be discussed at this review meeting.

Current curriculum provision

a.　　Within the classroom.

Enrichment extension activities identified in schemes and forecasts of work, which are then implemented and evaluated. There is recognition and utilization of children's abilities and talents, e.g. providing opportunities for a fluent, outgoing, articulate child to speak to class or school; talented child in technology to demonstrate his/her model.

This fits comfortably within the framework of the school's ethos which celebrates all children's activities and interests.

b.   In a small group or individually.

Working with others of like ability or with an adult, usually on a subject-specific activity. Exploring divergent and open-ended approaches to learning. We recognize that different starting points may be needed, and there should be flexibility. We plan work knowing that children may accelerate rapidly, and new concepts be grasped quickly.

c.   Out of school.

As with all our children, we build on out-of-school activities, e.g. music, dance, sport. We encourage contact with groups set up to support able children.

The role of the coordinator

We see this as crucial. The named person is a focus within the school – an enthusiastic, informed professional who with the headteacher has both an overview and specific knowledge of each child's abilities.

The coordinator is a consultant used by the class teacher. She (sic) in turn liaizes with colleagues, parents, outside agencies and receiving schools.

The coordinator also builds up resources, keeps abreast of current educational initiative and thinking, and plans specific schemes of work. She monitors and evaluates progress, and keeps records of achievement within and beyond the National Curriculum.

Parental involvement

We encourage parents to take an active part in their children's development, and share activities and progress with them both formally and informally. It is crucial to get to know the baseline for pupils on entry to the school.

Current resources

For younger children, a variety of material at a higher intellectual level.

IT adventure games and problem-solving activities.

SAT material as a guideline for the next level.

Cycle of review and development

Half-termly with class teacher, and at other times when necessary. Annually.

In-service

Special needs coordinator and headteacher report to staff on courses attended. Coordinator spends time with staff to evaluate progress and set individual targets for able children.

NAME	TGr	Form Tutor	Primary Head	AH2 (z-score)	Claus Urban	Bently	English	Mathematics	Science	German	French	History	Geography	R. Education	Music	Art	Drama	Phys Ed	Technology
Ian	BL			3.59	X	39	X	Ac		X		Ac		X					
John	RL			2.93		56	X	X											
Andrew	GM	X		2.75		42	X	X	X	X		X							
David	GM			2.27		43	X		X										
Lawrence	RL			2.09			X												
Donna	GL	X		2.09		45	X					X							
Adam	GM			2.03		39	X			Pr								Ac	
Graham	AL			2.03		38	X				X								
Ian	TL			1.01		52													
Iain	BL			1.61		52													
Gillian	RL			0.29		50			X			X			Ac				
Fern	HM			0.23		50			X										
Christine	GM	X		0.89		50	Ac								Ac				X
Benjamin	RM			1.55					X	X	X								
Dean	GL	X		1.73			X		Ac			X							
Natalie	RL			1.55		31			X										
Andrew	TM			1.91		44	X			X									
Rachael	RM			1.67		47	X			X									
Steven	RM			1.97		49	X			X									
Lisa	TL	X		1.31	X	44	X					X	X						
Louise	TL			1.85	X	42	X												
Gillian	GL	X		0.59		28				X									
Michael	GL			1.13						X									
Jeni	BL			1.55						X									
Alison	GM			1.19	X		X										Ac		
Andrew	GM			0.95	X														
Tom	BL			1.01			X				Ac	Ac			X				
Jonathan	TL			1.55	X														
Andrew	BL			0.77	X														
Kathleen	RL			0.83	X		X												
James	TL			1.25	X														
Michael	BL			1.49			X					Ac							
Amy	GM			1.31						Ac									
Brena	AL			0.53									Ac						
Stephen	HM			1.31				Ac											
Fern	HM			0.23													Ac		
Victoria	TL			1.49													Ac		
Kay	GM			0.11														Ac	

Ac indicates Achievement Certificate awarded
X indicates identified by staff

Note: Year 7 identification table from children nominated as being most able by their primary schools. No child seems to be gifted across the whole curriculum!

	Autumn	Term	Spring	Term	Summer	Term
KS2				Egg Race		
KS3 Year 7		Thinking Skills......		......	Newspaper	......>
Year 8	Thinking Skills......			......	......	......>
Year 9		Engineering		SATS		
KS4 Year 10				Money Management		River Study
Year 11				GCSE		Leadership
KS5 Year 12		Management		Young Consumer of the Year		
Year 13		A-Levels				

Notes   **BAYS/CREST? DUKE of ED?**

This event planner is to assist a support group of volunteer teachers to enter enrichment activities (vertical) to extension curriculum activities (horizontal) in a complementary way. Differentiated programmes for all is the aim.

Note: This matrix of activities indicates what action this successful school is taking over the year for the children identified. In addition to the curriculum time, children are expected to give one hour's additional homework per week, i.e. 40 hrs per year.

ACTION PLAN

SUBJECT: Identification of, and enrichment programme for able children

1. WHAT WE ARE DOING?	Identifying through AH2/3 test and AH5 in year 9 Setting in core and foundation subjects. Earling Entry in Mathematics and optional Stats.
2. WHAT NEEDS TO BE DONE?	1. Identify top 8% on entry, refine 2% 2. Identify specific talents. 3. Develop a programme of enrichment within subject areas. 4. Develop a complementary programme of enrichment cross curricular. 5. Develop a review process. 6. Develop a monitoring process.
3. HOW IT IS TO BE DONE?	1. AH2 primary feeders + others on entry. 2. Staff Questionnaire. Creativity and attribution measures. Primary school questionnaire. 3. HoD's to develop material and schemes of enhancement. Monitoring Strategies. Target KS3 level 7 KS4 level 10. Target Oxbridge. 4. **Enrichment** programme developed by support group. To consist of extra-curricular support and activities programmes for each Key Stage. 5. HoH/Programme director, standardised format to be agreed, for interviews and reports. 6. Links with HoD's Yr 9 test KSA's 3 & 4
4. SOURCES OF HELP AVAILABLE	1. NACE & NAGC. 2. LEA Special Needs/Psychological Serv' 3. Link with Nc University. 4. Link with BT, industry, armed service, mentors. 5. Parents
5. PROGRESS REVIEW.	Annual review of programme. **PI.** Record of progress/achievement, reports. **PI.** Collate data from departments. **PI.** Parent/pupil feedback sheet. **PI.** Staff questionnaire. **PI.** Schools Inspection Team Report. **PI.** Careers destinations and achievements.
6. EVALUATION	Carry out summative programme evaluation with the assistance of an outside agency/consultant after five years.
7. WHAT DO WE NEED TO DO NEXT?	Write development plan

Bognor Regis Community College

Identification of the most able

It was recognized that the most effective means of identifying pupils of high ability was through teacher assessment and recommendation. In addition, the primary liaising coordinator spends one afternoon each week in primary schools and as a result of this policy extra extension work is being set and marked for a small number of the most able pupils in Year six of the junior school. Also, accelerated entry is being negotiated for pupils of exceptional ability.

However, it was recognized also that many factors could inhibit classroom performance (e.g., social deprivation, trauma, psychological difficulties, frequent change of school, etc.) and the more objective indicators yielded by tests of basic cognitive ability were also regarded as important. Previously the Richmond Tests were used in Years seven and eight, and as specialist literature proved less than helpful in specifying or categorizing high ability special needs pupils, internal college categories were decided upon and the information disseminated to all members of staff who were asked to review the progress of and differentiated provision for such pupils, in the light of their potential as suggested by test scores.

Assessment revision

In the light of lessons learned from the process described above, the tests used for identification were thought to be over-complicated (11 separate sub-tests), lacking in a number of areas, e.g. no measure of spatial ability, and sexist. Hence, in the academic year 1991/2, Nelson's Cognitive Ability Tests were introduced (verbal, quantitative and non-verbal spatial), and set to Years seven and eight in the autumn term after a settling-in period. This data, plus the .... age score and a separate standardized Young's spelling test score provided the new information which was recategorized and issued to staff as a means of identifying special needs pupils.

Contact with parents

Following the analysis of CAT and associated tests, parents of the most able pupils of Year seven were invited to meet with the head teacher and the head of year to:

i.   agree an objective assessment of the pupil's ability and potential;
ii. share the home/school perspective in order to build up a profile of a pupil, both academic and pastoral;
iii. explore ways in which the parents could assist at home;
iv. agree an individual development programme for each pupil and targets set for the remainder of the year.

Quality control

All parents of Year seven pupils were issued with a quality questionnaire which proved extremely valuable in assessing the attitudes, perspective, and working hours of the most able pupils.

Examples of notes taken at parent interviews

Progress Report

The Principal reviewed the progress report and the CAT scores, pointing out that _____ was a year advanced and that this could have depressed the latter. Comments for mathematics and science were very good, could possibly be stretched more in science, but it appeared from the report that progress in English was not at the high level we would expect. _____ was reported to have fitted in well as a lower school librarian.

Parents' Comments

1. _____ has a clearcut threshold; if pushed hard he will switch off.
2. Can be shy; the actual teacher who takes the subject can make all the difference.
3. Grades good in science.
4. Has settled in well; problems with one other pupil: this was quickly resolved by the tutor.
5. Was originally getting bored in mathematics; situation better now he is using extension papers.
6. What will happen if he succeeds in the higher maths paper next year?
7. Less progress than expected in English; parents only aware of this when the teacher commented on it a few weeks ago.
8. Originally a little put off by rugby, had expected football, but after a while coped well. Likes badminton.
9. Objected to being called 'a boff'.
10. School had more than exceeded their expectations.

Friendships

_____ has tried hard with this aspect of his school life, and parents felt this was an area where he had considerably matured. His physical maturity had also moved forward in terms of PE activities and stature. A good mixer, but not a person who showed a need for particularly close friends.

Response to Parents' Comments

Teachers will be asked to keep a particularly careful check on performance in relation to ability. At the beginning his teachers would not have been aware of his ability in the way they are now. The matter of the higher maths paper will be considered in more detail next year.

Naturally objected to being called 'a boff'. Ways of handling this would be discussed with _____. Approach to friendships and general maturity very encouraging.

The Principal explained the three point grading system in science.

Action points

1. Year Tutor to check work in science and talk with teacher about the possibility of extra extension sheets.
2. Year Tutor to check English progress with English teacher and discuss this

with _____.

3. Year tutor to discuss overall work with _____ and the significance of `setting` in Year eight.

4. Year Tutor to inform the parents that _____ should make appointments as usual with regard to Year seven parents' evening.

Epilogue

'Come to the edge.'
  'We can't. We are afraid.'
'Come to the edge.'
  "We can't. We will fall.'
'Come to the edge.'
  And they came.
And he pushed them
  And they flew.

Appolinaire

'I have come to a frightening conclusion. I am the decisive element in the classroom. It is my personal approach that creates the climate. It is my daily mood that makes the weather. As a teacher I possess tremendous power to make a child's life miserable or joyous. I can be a tool of torture or an instrument of inspiration. I can humiliate or humour, hurt or heal. In all situations it is my response that decides whether a crisis will be escalated or de-escalated and a child humanized or de-humanized.'

Haim Ginott, Between Teacher and Child

Useful Addresses

Advisory Centre for Education Ltd
 1B Aberdeen Studios, 22/24 Highbury Grove, London
 N5 2EA
The Association for Science Education, College House,
 Hatfield AL10 9AA
The European Council for High Ability (Research)
 Building und Bedabung e.V., Wissenschaftszentrum, PO
 Box 20 14 48, D5300 Bonn 2, Germany
Foundation for Gifted Children
 5 Makepeace Avenue, London N6 6ELL
The Gifted Children's Information Centre
 Hampton Grange, Hampton Lane, Solihull
Gifted Education International
 AB Academic Publishers, PO Box 42, Bicester,
 Oxon OX6 7NW
The Mathematical Association
 295 London Road, Leicester LE2 3BE
Mensa Foundation for Gifted Children
 Mensa House, St John's Square,
 Wolverhampton WV2 4AH
National Association for Able Children in Education
 (NACE)
 Westminster College, Oxford OX2 9AT. Telephone
 01865 247644
The National Association for Gifted Children (NAGC)
 Elder House, Milton Keynes MK9 1LR.
National Association for Gifted Children (USA)
 1155, 15th Street NW, Suite 1002, Washington DC
 20055, USA – *(Gifted Child Quarterly Journal)*
The National Association for Special Educational Needs
 NASEN House, 4/5 Amber Business Village, Tamworth,
 Staffs B77 4RP
National Association for the Teaching of English, 50
 Broadfield Road, Broadfield Business Centre, Sheffield
 S8 0XJ
The National Council for Educational Technology
 (NCET)
 Sir W Lyons Road, Science Park, University of Warwick,
 Coventry CV4 7EZ
(Encourages supported self-study and has a consultancy
 and an information service)
NFER-Nelson (Tests)
 Derville House, 2 Oxford Road East, Windsor
Odyssey of the Mind – Mastery Education Corporation
85 Main Street, Waterwon, MA 02172, USA
Philosophy for Children
 Institute for the Advacement of Philosophy for
 Children, Montclair State College, Upper Montclair,
 NJ07043, USA

The Potential Trust
 7 Bateman Street, Headington, Oxford
Pullen Publications Limited
121 London Road, Knebworth, Herts SG3 6EX
(Produce enrichment and extension material)
Roeper Review
 PO Box 329, Bloomfield Hills, MI 48304, USA
Shell Education Service
 Shell UK Limited, Shell Mex House, Strand, London
 WC2R 0DX (Have produced a number of study
 projects related to industry, science and technology;
 these are available from Bankside House, West Mills,
 Newbury, Berks RG14 5HPP
World Council for Gifted and Talented Children
 The Belin-Blank Centre, College of Education, 210
 Linquist Centre, University of Iowa, Iowa City, IOWA
 52242–1529 (Journal – *Gifted Education*)

Glossary of Gifted and Talented Education (GATE) Definitions

Acceleration
> Refers to administrative practices designed to allow students to progress through the school at a rate faster than the average; e.g. early school entrance, content area acceleration, class-skipping, early examinations, but especially accelerated learning.

Appropriate pacing
> The content and pacing of curriculum and instruction are matched to students' abilities and needs. Students move ahead on the basis of mastery. Differentiation in pacing and/or depth is provided.

Cluster grouping
> Any classroom with a group of identified gifted/talented students purposefully organized to provide planned differentiated instruction most of the time, e.g. working on concept mapping.

Compacting
> This relieves children of boredom and repetitive learning of materials they already know – thus giving more time for exciting and challenging problems, etc. This requires questioning or testing to ensure mastery of a topic first and then the provision of new material.

Competitions
> Organized opportunities for gifted and talented students to enter local, regional or national contests in a variety of subject areas (e.g., Science Olympiad, Master Classes, Mars Art Competition).

Concurrent or dual enrolment
> Usually refers to secondary students taking some college courses at a nearby college or university before they leave school, but may also refer to students at any level who are allowed to take some classes at the next school level (e.g., infant/primary/secondary).

Correspondence courses
> Courses taken by correspondence through a college, university or other accrediting institution, e.g. Open University foundation courses.

Counselling
> Refers to planned activities, sessions, policies that assist gifted and talented students in planning their academic career in-school and after high school, and that also address specific social/emotional needs of the gifted – some parents as well!

Creative and productive thinking
> Divergent thinking that results in unconventional responses to conventional tasks.

Differentiation
> Children are all different, learn differently and therefore need a range of teaching and learning styles. Differentiation can be by: outcome; rate of progress; enrichment; and by setting different tasks. Differentiation is accessing the whole curriculum to the learning needs of the individual.

Enrichment class
> A group organized from one or more classrooms, which meets on a regular basis to provide experiences beyond the established curriculum.

Enrichment in the regular classroom
> Experiences provided to broaden horizons and experience in the regular classroom that are additional and/or supplemental to the established curriculum and/or texts and which are purposefully planned with the needs, interests, and capabilities of particular students in mind. Certainly not more of the same.

Extension
> To move children in depth to higher order thinking, concepts and attitudes.

Independent study
> Individually contracted in-depth study of a topic which many able students want.

Interest groups
> Any group organized from one or more classrooms on the basis of interest in a topic; usually short-term in duration, possibly out of school hours in an Explorers Club or NAGC Saturday Club.

International Baccalaureate
> A rigorous, comprehensive programme that enhances and extends the quality of the 11th and 12th year course offerings. The internationally recognised IB curriculum provides students with a comprehensive background in English, a foreign

language, the social sciences, physical and life sciences, mathematics and the arts. The IB diploma is accepted at many foreign universities and at colleges.

Mentorship
A programme which pairs individual students with someone who has advanced skills and experiences in a particular discipline and can serve as a guide, adviser, counsellor, and role model. Careful selection and matching is essential.

Ongoing assessment
Students' abilities and needs are continually assessed through both formal and informal means designed to discover and nurture talent. The results are used as the basis for appropriate programming decisions. This also helps to prevent underachievement. Records of achievement are a good example of long-term holistic profiling of a child.

Problem solving
Encouraging children to think convergently and divergently to tackle real open-ended problems in which they delight. These range from problems in school to problems of the world and the future. The process includes problem finding, solution finding and acceptance.

Resource room
Students are released from their regular classroom on a scheduled basis to work with a teacher or mentor specializing in education of the gifted in a resource-room setting.

Seminars, workshops
Special short-term sessions where the student focuses on one area of study (e.g., Young Authors Conference, Maths and Science Master Classes).

Underachievement
The difference between what a child actually achieves and could achieve.

Bibliography

Bentley. A. (19) *Music Test*, Routledge, London.

Binet, A. (1985) *The Education of Intelligence*, F E Peacock, Itasca, IL.

Bloom, B.S. (1982) 'The role of gifts in the development of talent', *Exceptional Children*, 48 (6).

Bloom, B.S. (1985) *Developing Talent in Young People*, Ballantine Books, New York.

Braggett, E.J. (1992) *Pathways for Accelerated Learners*, Hawker Brownlow, Sydney.

Butler-Por, N. (1987) *Gifted Underachievers*, John Wiley, Chichester.

Clark, B. (1988) *Growing Up Gifted*, Merrill, Columbus.

Coleman, L. (1985), *Schooling the Gifted*, Addison-Wesley, Reading, Mass.

Colengelo, W.L. and Davis, G.A. (1991) *Handbook of Gifted Education*, Allyn & Bacon, New York.

Czikszentmihalyi, M. Rathunde, K. and Wholen, S. (1993). *Talented Teenagers – The Roots of Success and Failure*, Cambridge, Cambridge University Press.

Davis, G.A. and Rimm, S.B. (1989) *Education of the Gifted and Talented*, Prentice Hall, New York.

DES (1992) *The Education of Very Able Children in Maintained Schools*, HMSO, London.

DfE Circulars 4/93 and 5/93, HMSO, London.

Denton, C. and Postlethwaite, K. (1985) *Able Children*, NFER-Nelson, Windsor.

Dunn, R., Dunn, K. and Treffinger, D. (1992) *Bringing Out the Giftedness in the Young Child*, John Wiley, Chichester.

Edwards, B. (1992) *Drawing on the Right Side of the Brain*, Harper Collins, London.

Essex County Council (1993) *Guidelines for Secondary Schools for Effective Differentiation in the Classroom*, Essex Education Department.

Eyre, D. and Marjoram, T.D. (1990) *Enriching and Extending the National Curriculum*, Kogan Page, London.

Feldhusen, J. (1994) 'Talent identification and development in education', *Gifted Education International*, vol. 10.

Fisher, R. (1992) *Teaching Children to Think*, Simon and Schuster, Hemel Hempstead.

Gaarder, J. (1996) *Sophie's World*, Phoenix, London.

Gallagher, J.J. (1985) *Teaching the Gifted Child*, Allyn & Bacon, New York.

Galton, F. (1869) *Hereditary Genius*, Macmillan, London.

Gardner, H. (1983) *Frames of Mind*, Basic Books, New York.

George, D.R. (1992) *The Challenge of the Able Child*, David Fulton, London.

George, D.R. (1993) 'Instructional strategies and models for gifted education', in *Research and Development of Giftedness and Talent* (Heller, K.A. Monks, F.J. and Passow, H.A., eds), Pergamon Press, Oxford.

George, D.R. (1994) *Enrichment Activities for More Able Children*, Chalkface, Milton Keynes.

Goleman, D. (1996) *Emotional Intelligence*, Bloomsbury, London.

Gross, M.U.M. (1993) *Exceptionally Gifted Children*, Routledge, London.

Guildford, J.P. (1967) *The Nature of Human Intelligence*, McGraw-Hill, New York.

Handy, C. (1994) *The Empty Raincoat*, Hutchinson, London.

Harvey, S. and Steeley, J. (1984) 'An investigation into relationships among intelligence, creative abilities, extra curricular activities, achievement and giftedness in a delinquent population, *Gifted Children Quarterly*, 28.

Herrman, N. (1988) *The Creative Brain*, Brain Books, North Carolina.

Kerry, T. (1983) *Finding and Helping the Able Child*, Croom Helm, Beckenham.

Leyden, S. (1985) *Helping the Child of Exceptional Ability*, Routledge, London.

Li, R. (1996) *A Theory of Conceptual Intelligence*, Praeger, USA.

Maslow, A.H. (1954) *Motivation and Personality*, Harper and Row, New York.

NFER-Nelson (1994) *Educational Assessment. The Way Ahead*, NFER-Nelson, Windsor.

OFSTED (1993) *Exceptionally Able Children*, DfE, London.

Ogilvie, E. (1973) *Gifted Children in Primary Schools*, Macmillan, London.

Pegnato, C. and Birch, J. (1959) 'Locating gifted children in junior high schools', *Exceptional Children*, 25.

Renzulli, J.S. and Hartman, R.. (1971) 'Scale for rating the behavioural characteristics of superior students', *Exceptional Children*, 38(3).

Renzulli, J.S. (1977) *The Enrichment Triad Model: A Guide for Developing Defensible Programs for the Gifted and Talented*, Creative Learning Press, USA.

Renzulli, J.S. (1988) *The Multiple Menu Model for Developing Differentiated Curriculum for the Gifted and Talented*, University of Connecticut, USA.

Renzulli, J.S. and Reiz, S.M. (1991) 'The reform movement and the quiet crisis in gifted education', *Gifted Child Quarterly*, 35(1).

Saunders, L., Stradling, R. and Weston P. (1992) *Differentiation in Practice*, DES-NFER, HMSO, London.

Shore, B.M. (1991) 'Building a professional knowledge base', *Exceptionality Education*, 1(1).

Sisk, D. (1987) *Creative Teaching of Gifted*, McGraw Hill, New York.

Straker, A. (1983) *Mathematics for Gifted Pupils*, Longman, Harlow.

Teare, J.B. (1988) A *School Policy on Provision for Able Pupils*, NACE, Northampton.

Terman, L.M. and Oden, M.H. (1947) *Genetic Study of Genius*, Stanford University Press, Stanford, CA.

Torrence, E.P. (1980) 'Assessing the further reaches of creative potential', *Journal of Creative Behaviour*, 14.

Urban, K. and Jellen, H. (1995) *Test for Creative Thinking – Drawing Production*, SWETS Test Services, Lisse, The Netherlands.

Young, P. and Tyre, C. (1992) *Gifted or Able – Realizing Children's Potential*, Open University Press, Milton Keynes.

£14.00   7/2000